Bathroom Makeovers

GW00705968

Julian Cassell
Peter Parham

MARSHALL PUBLISHING · LONDON

A Marshall Edition
Conceived, edited and designed by
Marshall Editions
The Orangery
161 New Bond Street
London W1Y 9PA

First published in the UK in 2000 by
Marshall Publishing Ltd

ISBN: 1-84028-378-5

Originated in Singapore by Chroma Graphics.
Printed and bound in China by Excel Printing.

Project Editor Felicity Jackson
Designed by Martin Lovelock
       & John Round
Photographer Tim Ridley
Illustrations Chris Forsey
Project Manager Nicholas Barnard
Managing Art Editor Patrick Carpenter
Managing Editor Antonia Cunningham
Editorial Director Ellen Dupont
Art Director Dave Goodman
Editorial Coordinator Ros Highstead
Production Anna Pauletti
Indexer Hilary Bird

Front cover photography: **Tim Ridley** (top left,
centre and bottom centre) **John Freeman** (top
right) **R. Honeyset/ Arcaid** (bottom left) **Paul
Ryan/ International Interiors** (bottom right)
Back cover photography: **Tim Ridley**

Note

Every effort has been taken to ensure that all
information in this book is correct and compatible with
national standards generally accepted at the time of
publication. This book is not intended to replace the
manufacturer's instructions in the use of their tools or
materials – always follow their safety guidelines. The
author and publisher disclaim any liability, loss, injury or
damage incurred as a consequence, directly or indirectly,
of the use and application of the contents of this book.

*The authors would like to
thank the following
companies for their
assistance in producing this
book:*

Bliss
Paradise Works
Arden Forest Estate
Alcester, Warwickshire
B49 6EH
Tel. 0870 0110800

Fired Earth
South Street
Sherborne Dorset
DT9 3TD
Tel. 01935 817900

S M Flooring
65 Cheap Street
Sherborne, Dorset
DT9 3BA
Tel. 01935 815575

Dulux Decorator Centres
Altrincham, Cheshire
WA14 5PG
Tel. 0161 9683000

The DEVA Tap Company
Brooklands Mill
English Street. Leigh
Lancashire
WN7 3EH
Tel. 01942 680177

Dave Marsh Hardware
Fore Street
Castle Cary, Somerset
BA7 7BG
Tel. 01963 350316

The English Stamp
Company
Worth Matravers, Dorset
BH19 3JP
Tel. 01929 439117

The Stencil Store
89 Lower Sloane Street
London
SW1 W8DA
Tel. 0171 823 6700

Polyvine Ltd
Vine House, Rockhampton
Berkeley, Gloucestershire
GL13 9DT
Tel. 01454 261276

Tile Wise Ltd
12-14 Enterprise Mews
Sea King Road
Lynx Trading Estate, Yeovil
Somerset
BA20 2NZ
Tel. 01935 412220

B J White
4 Vale Road
Pen Mill Trading Estate
Yeovil, Somerset
BA21 5HL
Tel. 01935 382400

Sharpe & Fisher (BS) Ltd
Mill Street
Wincanton, Somerset
BA9 9AP
Tel. 01963 33881

The Tile Market
Bardell Court
Houndstone Business Park
Yeovil, Somerset
Tel. 01935 433331

Hewden Plant Hire
Station Road
Bruton, Somerset
BA10 0EH
Tel. 01749 812267

Bruton Doll1s House &
Miniatures Co
Station Road
Bruton, Somerset
BA10 0EH

B J Haigh-Lumby
1 High Street
Castle Cary, Somerset
BA7 7AN
Tel. 01963 351259

MGR Exports
Station Road
Bruton, Somerset
BA10 0EH
Tel. 01749 812460

*Further thanks goes to the
following individuals who
supplied props and general
assistance:*

Adele Parham, Emma
Isaacs, Katriena Veal, Carol
Clements, Jakki Dearden,
Ann Clothier, Rob
Mahoney, and Julia
Barnard.

All styling for set
photography by Julian
Cassell, Peter Parham, Tim
Ridley and Katrina Moore.

CONTENTS

INTRODUCTION

The bathroom is the one area of the home that provides a great opportunity to experiment with a large number of finishes – you can indulge yourself creating a look that satisfies all your needs and aspirations. A bathroom makeover can range from changing the taps to total refitting and redecoration – both approaches, carried out properly, can be equally successful in producing a finish you can be really proud of.

Because the bathroom is one of the most used rooms in the house, most of us like to create a comfortable and homely atmosphere that fits in with the rest of the household decoration. The main thing to remember is that the bathroom decoration must be practical and able to withstand the rigours of everyday use, as well as attractive and stylish. All the instructions for decorative finishes in this book keep these facts in mind, showing you how to deal with the main bathroom drawback – moist air and all the unpleasant problems it can cause. The book also explains how standard decorating techniques can be adjusted to create more hard-wearing, water-repellent finishes.

DESIGNING FOR THE SPACE

Whether you are deciding on the colour scheme or designing storage facilities, always take the size of the room into account – bathrooms are often small rooms. From a purely decorative angle, it is easier to choose colours for a small room as swatches of paint on the walls can give a very good impression of the effect that colour will have, whereas a swatch in a larger room with vast expanses of wall tends to get overshadowed. This also applies to samples of fabric, wallpaper, tiles and floor coverings. Make good use of samples provided by retailers before making any final decisions and always look at the samples in the bathroom itself, so that the different colours, textures and finishes can be seen in the actual surroundings they will be used in.

CLEVER STORAGE

Since bathrooms tend to be one of the smaller rooms in the house, it is essential that you utilize all available space. Making the best use of space requires imaginative, well-designed storage systems. The secret is to try and provide functional areas that also have lots of decorative appeal and add to the look of the room as a whole. Chapter 1 is full of creative ideas for all those essential bathroom items – places to store them or just display them, tailored and finished to your specific needs.

BATHROOM DECORATING

To a certain extent, the systems and techniques used for decorating a bathroom differ very little from those methods used for other rooms in the home, but there are some extra considerations. Chapter 2 provides excellent, foolproof instruction on decorating technique as a whole and also discusses variations and different ideas that are particularly suited to a bathroom rather than other areas of the home.

DEALING WITH FLOORS

Floor space is limited in most bathrooms so it is important to choose the correct floor covering, paying particular attention to its practical qualities as well as its decorative appeal. Chapter 3 explains all the suitable options for bathroom floors, with step-by-step directions on how to create the look you require and the most appropriate techniques for achieving it.

FITTING DETAILS

The accessories that turn a bathroom into a practical and functional room include things like the lighting, blinds and mirrors. These are just a few of the examples found in Chapter 4, all of which combine to provide the finishing touches to a bathroom makeover. Take time to consider the mood you want to create, and the style requirements this will involve, before you choose the accessories, since this will help you achieve the kind of bathroom you want.

PLUMBING AWARENESS

It is well worth every householder being aware of how their plumbing system works and where any potential problems may occur, because not all areas of plumbing need to be left to the professionals. Chapter 5 shows you how to tackle some of the simpler plumbing jobs that can help you to make changes in bathroom systems for both practical and decorative reasons. Understanding how your bathroom plumbing functions helps you to decide whether you need to call in a professional plumber when you are doing a complete or partial bathroom makeover.

MAKING CHANGES

Changing the look of your bathroom can be an ongoing process – you may jump forward in very large leaps, or progress slowly with small, well-thought-out improvements that gradually build up to a completely different atmosphere and finish. Chapter 6 provides lots of ideas for this sort of gradual progression and for those final touches, the last little details needed to complete the bathroom makeover.

ENJOYING A MAKEOVER

Decorating is a very rewarding pastime, producing a definite result that can be enjoyed every day. Add to this all the other activities associated with a bathroom makeover and you have a complete extra dimension – bathroom makeovers should never be thought of as a laborious task, because the pleasure derived from the finished product is well worth all the effort. Always remember to spend as much time planning a makeover as actually carrying it out; having a clear set of guidelines and an order of work helps to direct you through the various processes in the correct order to complete the job satisfactorily. This book is the essential guide for all home decorators, whatever the level of aptitude, providing plenty of ideas and instruction to help you to produce designs and finishes for your home, to enjoy now and for many years to come.

GENERAL TOOLS

A basic household toolbox is essential for carrying out bathroom makeovers, as there are some tools you will need time and time again during the process. Not all the tools shown here will be required at once, so it is important to prioritize and build up a larger toolbox over the years, until you are capable of dealing with every eventuality.

Hot-air gun

Chisels

Electrical tape

Adjustable spanner

Tape measure

Profile gauge

Bolster chisel

Sander

Workbench

Dust mask

Staple gun

Torpedo level

Panel saw

Cordless drill/driver

Hacksaw

Jigsaw

Hammer

Plastering float

Stepladder

Mitre block

Scot-head screwdrivers

Cross-head screwdrivers

Plier wrench

DECORATING TOOLS

I t is important to have a good selection of tools available to carry out the required decorations in the bathroom. Choose the items carefully, making sure that they are good value for money and capable of producing the best finish. More expensive equipment tends to be the best quality, producing excellent results and lasting long enough to be used for other decorating projects.

Masking tape

Craft knife

Natural sponge

Sponge

Graining comb

Paint pad and application bracket

Cotton rag

Stamps

Pasting brush

Paper-hanging brush

Paper-hanging scissors

Stencil brush

Window scraper

Paintbrushes

Fitch

Tile saw

Sealant dispenser

Protective gloves

Roller cage and sleeve

Grout spreader

Mitre saw

Large notched spreader

Shavehook

Filling knife

Clever Storage

CLEVER STORAGE

Generally bathrooms are one of the smaller rooms in the home, with limited floor space that can restrict freedom of movement. Despite its size, however, the bathroom is still very busy and needs plenty of storage space. Towels, toiletries and all manner of ornaments and decorative accessories require either a place to keep them or somewhere to display them. The secret of clever storage in bathrooms is to create as much space as possible through the design of the storage systems, using areas otherwise considered as wasted space, as well as keeping them attractive, so that they are decorative items rather than functional eyesores.

DECIDING ON STORAGE AREAS

There are all sorts of factors to consider when choosing bathroom storage. You have to decide how practical these areas need to be and balance it with their decorative appeal. House size as a whole is important – in many cases the airing cupboard and storage space for toiletries must be included in the bathroom. Where these can be built in other parts of the house, storage in the bathroom becomes less vital and decorative shelving and display areas can be more important.

Combining storage and style: open shelving allows for both storage and display; it is a very practical way of housing items vital to bathroom activities and combines this function with an ordered look, keeping things close at hand and easy to find.

Practical storage: any well-designed shelving is an excellent space-saving facility, making use of otherwise wasted areas of the bathroom, and accommodating lots of items in a relatively small space.

The built-in approach: a neat, compact finish is easy to achieve if you have a number of built-in units. These units maximize storage while minimizing space wastage. Professional help may be required to produce a perfect custom-made finish, although many retailers do sell 'flat-packed' cupboard and shelving systems that are relatively simple to assemble and fit.

Maintaining ventilation: bathrooms are prone to high levels of moisture in the air, so it is essential to keep them well ventilated. This is a vital consideration with the storage facilities – having cupboard doors that allow air to circulate is very helpful, especially in smaller bathrooms.

STORAGE IDEAS

- Displaying and concealing: it is always a good idea to have some storage areas that can be used to show off attractive items, but it is equally important to have unobtrusive cupboards and shelving for storing items that do not necessarily warrant open viewing.
- Child-proofing: medicines are often kept in bathroom cabinets and these

cabinets should be positioned out of the reach of children and, if possible, have a lock on them.
- Dual purpose: combining functions is the secret of clever storage; for example, a wall cabinet containing a mirror or a shelf with hooks on the underneath are prime examples of maximizing space by having one item fulfil two jobs.

USING CORNERS

C orners are often wasted areas of a room, especially in bathrooms, where basins and other fittings prevent larger pieces of furniture from being positioned in corners. Storage systems tend to require fixing into the corner itself, rather than having a fixed base. All kinds of corner units can be bought from retailers but, using a few simple ideas, you can create clever designs of your own, such as tile shelving.

TILE SHELVING

Tiles are often used to form shelved areas in bathrooms, but this is normally confined to bath ledges or on a windowsill. A more innovative use is to just use the tiles themselves, as single shelves in their own right. Large floor tiles are ideal for this purpose and can be used to create novel corner shelving.

| Mark a diagonal line from corner to corner across a floor tile, using a piece of batten for a straight edge. Use a tile cutter to cut two identical triangular shapes from the floor tile.

2 Hold the tile, wrong side down, at the required level in the corner and adjust its position until it is level. Mark with a pencil on the wall along the underside of the tile.

3 Hold a jointing block just below the pencil line and drill two pilot holes. Depending on the wall, you may need wall plugs in order to get a firm fixing for the screws.

4 Screw in the jointing block then position another close to it. Position two more blocks on the adjacent wall.

5 Place a tile on the blocks and apply a gloss or matt varnish to the cut edge of the tile, depending on the finish required. The shelves can be left unfixed so that they can be removed easily. Alternatively, to make each shelf more secure, some adhesive can be applied to the top of each jointing block before the tile is placed in position.

ADDING MORE SHELVES
Add more shelves to the corner as required. Since the jointing blocks are small enough to hide how the tiles are fixed, they do not detract from the look of this 'suspended' tile shelving.

PRACTICAL CORNER STORAGE

C orner spaces are ideal for use as practical storage areas. These will add to the decoration of the room while making maximum use of this space. They also give you the opportunity to test your skills by building across the corner and creating open storage systems. Precise measurements and accurate cutting are essential if you want to produce excellent results.

MAKING A TOWEL STACK

Bathrooms are always full of towels and these are often hidden away in airing cupboards. Displaying them gives you the chance to make an otherwise dull storage system far more attractive, and keeping them in the open means they are well ventilated and within easy reach.

1 Measure out 45 cm (18 in) from the corner and draw a level line from this point back to the corner.

2 Cut a 45 cm (18 in) length of 5 x 1 cm (2 x ½ in) batten, mitring one end.

3 Attach the batten above the pencil line, using two masonry nails, with the mitred end pointing away from the corner. Attach a corresponding batten, 44 cm (17½ in) in length, on the adjacent wall. Measure the distance between the end point of the mitre on each wall, and cut another length of batten to this size, mitring the cuts so that the ends of the batten will fit snugly against the wall.

4 Nail the batten in place with panel pins. Continue to fit further battens along the top of the frame, measuring 2 cm (¾ in) along the wall towards the corner for each new length.

5 Cut a 30 cm (12 in) length of batten and nail it vertically, set below and slightly back from the corner of the first horizontal batten. Add three more battens at equal distances to the corner. Repeat these vertical lengths on the adjacent wall.

6 Repeat steps 1-4 to produce another horizontal slatted platform below the vertical battens. Finish the wood with varnish or colour rub with an emulsion, as shown here. Leave the paint to dry then seal the wood with a coat of varnish. Allow it to dry before use.

COLOURFUL AND ELEGANT
A towel stack creates a colourful and elegant piece of practical shelving.

SIMPLE SHELVES

S omething simple is often the most effective kind of shelving. There is no specific design for a simple shelf, except that it should be as uncomplicated as possible and provide enough support for the objects it will hold. Make sure that the finished shelf is level on the wall and choose a finish that will complement the decorative style of the room.

1 On a length of 12.5 x 2.5cm (5 x 1 in) softwood measure 6 cm (2½ in) in from each corner. Draw lines at right angles to these marks to make a cross then use a paint can to draw three curves in a bracket shape.

2 Use a jigsaw to cut along the curved pencil guideline. Follow the manufacturer's safety instructions when using a jigsaw, and never stand in front of the blade. Repeat steps 1 and 2 to make a second bracket.

3 Cut another length of 12.5 x 2.5 cm (5 x 1 in) prepared softwood to the required length for your shelf. Hold a bracket 12.5 cm (5 in) in from the cut end, drawing a pencil guideline along the point where the bracket meets the shelf.

4 Hold the bracket securely on the guideline and drill a pilot hole through the bracket into the shelf.

5 Fix a screw into the hole (see below), making sure that it bites firmly into the shelf, but does not go all the way through to what will be the shelf surface. For extra strength, apply some wood glue to the bracket before positioning it by the guideline. Attach the other bracket to the shelf in the same way.

6 Drill another hole in each bracket for wall fixing. Position the shelf using a level, then screw through the brackets into the wall, using wall plugs, if necessary. For added strength, drill and fix two screws at a 45 degree angle through the top of the shelf (at the back), through the brackets and into the wall. Fill all screw holes. Round the corners of the shelf with sandpaper.

DECORATIVE
STORAGE SYSTEM
Once decorated, a
simple shelf provides an
attractive decorative
storage system for
ornaments or items in
everyday use.

FIXING THE SCREWS

Use a countersink drill bit to open up the entrance to the drilled hole on the bracket, so that the screw will fit below the wood surface.

WALL-SUSPENDED SHELVES

A llowing the majority of the weight of a shelf to be supported from above, rather than from below, produces an interesting effect that is different from the more traditional shelves. Combining wood with rope, and using large, obvious wall fixings, all adds to the sturdy, uncomplicated design of a wall-suspended shelf. The rustic appeal of this kind of design lends itself to a very natural-looking finish, such as waxing, a distressed paint effect or a simple colour rub.

1 Use a piece of 12.5 x 2.5 cm (5 x 1 in) planed softwood for your shelf – here cut to 60 cm (2 ft). Cut a piece of 2 cm (¾ in) quadrant beading to the same length. Screw the quadrant into the wall at the required shelf height, using a torpedo level to make sure the quadrant is level. Drill pilot holes and insert wall plugs, if necessary, for a good fixing.

2 Measure 2.5 cm (1 in) in from the edge of the shelf, and 7.5 cm (3 in) from its end, and make a pencil mark. Drill a hole at this mark, using a bit of a similar size to the rope being used to support the shelf – a diameter of 7.5 mm (⅓ in) is ideal. Make another hole in the corresponding position at the other end of the shelf.

3 Cut two lengths of rope to about 45 cm (18 in) long. Thread one piece through each hole in the shelf and tie each piece with a knot on the underneath, as shown.

4 Position the shelf above the quadrant on the wall, making sure that the edge of the shelf is tight up against the wall/quadrant junction. Screw in three wood screws at equal distances along the back edge of the shelf, going through the shelf and into the quadrant below.

5 In a vertical line from the drilled rope holes, screw two large 'eye' brackets into the wall about 25 cm (10 in) above the shelf. If necessary, drill a pilot hole before using a screwdriver as a lever to screw the 'eye' into the wall. Once both 'eyes' are in position, thread the two loose ends of the rope through their corresponding 'eye', and tie them so that the rope is taut.

NATURAL LOOK
This shelf has been finished with a white liming wax to protect and decorate the wood, while maintaining its natural look.

CEILING-SUSPENDED SHELVES

S helving can be designed to hang from the ceiling, rather than using the wall as the main weight support. For this kind of shelving, it is essential to find a strong fixing point – a solid wooden joist – as the entire weight of the hanging shelf is taken by this one point. However, once this obstacle is overcome, suspended ceiling shelving creates an excellent effect, giving you secure shelving without any cumbersome supports. Three shelves are ideal for creating a balanced looking shelving system.

1 Cut three 45 cm (18 in) lengths from 12.5 x 2.5cm (5 x 1 in) planed softwood. At one end of each length, screw in two small 'eyes', 12 mm (½ in) from the edge. Screw in two 'eyes' at the other end of each shelf in the corresponding position.

2 Using wirecutters, cut four pieces of chain each measuring 90 cm (3 ft) in length.

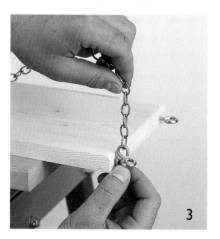

3 Attach the bottom link of one chain to each of the four 'eyes' on one of the shelves, using chain hooks. Measure 20 cm (8 in) up each chain and position another shelf, and finally measure the same distance again and position the final shelf. On the chain shown here, 20 cm (8 in) is the same as 20 links of the chain, which is an easy way of measuring between 'eyes'.

4

5

4 To find a firm fixing point in the ceiling, make a number of holes with an old screwdriver or bradawl until you find a solid wooden joist. Try and find a fixing position no more than 7.5 cm (3 in) away from the wall, so that the shelf will gain some small support from the wall to prevent it from spinning round.

5 Screw a large hook into the fixing hole. Use a screwdriver as leverage to make sure that the hook is solidly screwed into place. Fill in the other holes. Take the four loose ends of chain and position the final link of each four over the hook, adjusting the chains into the correct position, if necessary.

SUSPENDING SHELVES
Once in place, all the effort of suspending shelving is well worthwhile. A simple, coloured stain is the ideal way of finishing the shelves to create a stunning suspended shelving system.

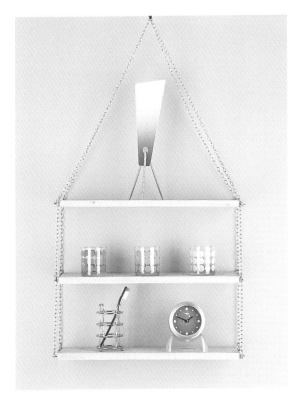

RACKS AND RAILS

S helves and traditional bathroom rails can be adapted to give them a more innovative appearance, while still maintaining their use as storage facilities. Playing with ideas can be great fun, allowing for freedom of expression and the chance to try something new.

TOOTHBRUSH MUG RACK

The idea of a toothbrushmug rack is by no means new, but some simple design changes, such as keeping the shelf very angular, and decorating it with something like metallic paint, can give it an ultra-modern look. For the design below, the toothmug must have a larger rim than base.

1 Cut a length of 12.5 x 2.5 cm (5 x 1 in) planed softwood to the required length, allowing for two triangular brackets to be cut from this length. Hold a toothbrush mug central to the shelf's depth, but to one side of its width, and draw a guideline.

2 Use a jigsaw to cut out both brackets. Drill a hole at the edge of the circular pencil guideline to accommodate the jigsaw blade, and cut out the central area. Attach the brackets and the shelf to the wall.

SIMPLISTIC
This simplistic rack can be painted to match any colour scheme and will look perfectly at home in any modern bathroom.

TOWEL RAILS

A novel towel rail can be produced from simple copper pipes of the type normally used for carrying water around the home. By combining straight lengths of pipe with right-angled joints and T-shaped connectors, it is possible to create all sorts of shapes and designs. Use a proprietary adhesive capable of securing two metal surfaces to stick the joints together.

I Decide on the dimensions of the towel rail you require then cut lengths of pipe to size. Pipe cutters can be used, but a sharp hacksaw will do the job just as efficiently.

2 Glue elbow joints and T connectors to the pipe lengths, making sure that there is a strong bond. Wipe off any excess adhesive before it dries.

3 Drill holes through the T connectors that back onto the wall surface. Fix them in place on the wall before the rest of the framework is built up, to give the finished rail no visible fixing points. Before using, coat the rail with a good-quality varnish to prevent damp towels from corroding the copper, and the towels themselves from becoming stained.

SLOPING FRAMEWORK
On this design, the three lengths of pipe become increasingly smaller as they go down the rack. When towels are hung on each level, they miss the towel below, which allows them to dry faster.

BATH HATCHES

T here are often areas at the foot or head of a bath that are under-used and waste their space-saving capabilities. Instead of totally boxing in these areas, you can fit a door in the boxing and use the space as storage cupboards. Bath hatches need to be fitted according to the specific design of your bath (see opposite); however, there are certain points that must be considered before building any such storage system.

HINGED HATCHES

It is essential that hatch doors fit precisely and their hinging mechanism ensures that the door sits flush. Use the aptly named 'flush' hinges – these hinges are relatively easy to fit and run all the way along the hinged edge of the hatch, making a very precise finish to the door edge.

1 Cut the bath hatch to the right size and clamp it vertically in a workbench. Cut the flush hinge to length, using a hacksaw, and hold the hinge along the appropriate edge of the hatch, marking the screw positions with a pencil.

2 Remove the hinge and drill pilot holes at the pencil marks on the hatch.

3 Hold the hinge along the edge, and fix it in place with the appropriate size screws. Holding the hinged hatch in place, mark the position for the corresponding hinge holes, drill the pilot holes and screw the hinge in position.

TOP ACCESS HATCH

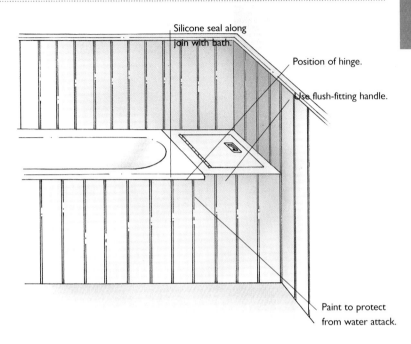

Silicone seal along join with bath.

Position of hinge.

Use flush-fitting handle.

Paint to protect from water attack.

SIDE ACCESS

Leave the door untiled, as tiling restricts hinge movement.

Position of hinge.

Fit magnetic catch to keep door closed.

HOOKS AND PEGS

Hooks and pegs are ideal for hanging towels, bathrobes and general bathroom bits and pieces. Hooks are usually positioned on the back of doors, or out of the way in corners and alcoves. However, with some smooth dowel and planed softwood you can make a wooden peg rack attractive enough to take pride of place in your bathroom.

1 Cut a 60 cm (2 ft) length of 12.5 × 2.5 cm (5 × 1 in) planking and then divide it into five equal sections 12 cm (4⅘ in) wide, marking each section with a pencil guideline. Bisect the pencil lines with a central guideline along the length of the plank.

2 Using a drill bit that corresponds to the size of dowel you are using, drill into the plank at the pencil-line cross-sections. Hold the drill at a slight angle and keep it consistent for all four holes. Try not to allow it to go all the way through the plank.

3 Using a saw, cut four lengths of wooden dowel, each measuring 15 cm (6 in) long.

4 Apply a generous amount of wood glue to one end of each wooden dowel.

5 Carefully insert one dowel into each of the drilled holes in the plank of wood.

6 Remove any excess glue with a cloth before it dries. Allow the peg rack to dry completely before painting it.

BATHROOM ESSENTIALS
Once painted and fixed to the wall, this wooden peg rack makes an attractive storage system that is ideal for hanging all manner of bathroom essentials.

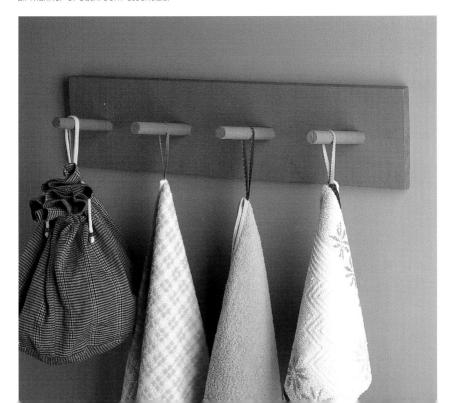

BASIN STORAGE

The area around basins is often wasted as far as storage space is concerned. Creating a vanity unit is one option for utilizing this area. A more simplistic approach is to make a curtain divide. This can easily be blended in with other soft furnishings in the room, and the decoration as a whole. All that is required is some self-adhesive touch-and-close tape and either one or two curtains to fit the required area.

1 Unroll a section of touch-and-close tape and stick one side of it around the edge of the basin, about 5 cm (2 in) from the rim of the basin. Although the basin profile makes it difficult to keep the tape smooth and level, try to avoid creases and keep it as parallel to the rim as possible. Any small undulations will be covered by the curtain.

2 Attach the other side of the touch-and-close tape to the back of the curtain or curtains, and then carefully press it onto the tape on the basin until it adheres. This method of attachment means it is very easy to remove the curtain for cleaning.

VANITY UNIT

A vanity unit is a more complicated form of basin storage, which requires a great deal more planning and considerable fitting skills. However, the end product looks extremely attractive while creating a practical, hidden storage system.

DECORATING WALLS

The decoration of a bathroom usually plays the most important part in giving the room its overall look, and colours and finishes need to be carefully considered. General decorating ideas apply in the normal way, but some practical requirements must be taken into consideration. Bathroom activities make tiles ideal for some of the wall surfaces, while paper and paint should be chosen with due regard for their hard-wearing properties. This chapter explains how surfaces should be prepared and how decorating materials are applied to make them suitable for bathroom use.

CHOOSING A STYLE

A bathroom is often dominated by one particular type of decorating material, which may be tiles, paper or paint. If there is a strong theme, other features in the room need to complement this. The secret of a pleasing decorative look is to get the balance right between the main theme and the smaller details, and produce a well coordinated finished product.

Papering: wallpapering is the easiest way to create an instant pattern, as well as providing texture and warmth in what can be a small and cramped room. Vinyl papers are best in bathrooms as they are hard-wearing and wipeable. It is doubly important in a bathroom to make sure that the paper is well stuck down, especially around the edges and along the seams.

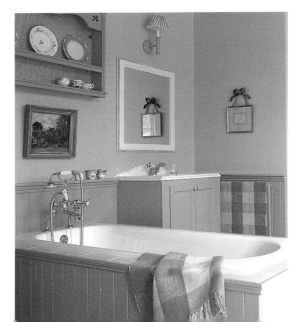

Painting walls: the look of a bathroom can be transformed very easily and quickly by painting the walls. Woodwork can then be painted to match the walls – with the enormous range of colours available, it is not difficult to find just the colour you want. Shades of blue always work well as they tend to provide a clean and fresh feel that balances well with the bathroom environment.

Dominating with tiles: tiles are always a very practical decorative material to use in a bathroom – extremely easy to keep clean and very hard-wearing. A tiled theme can produce an impressive, highly decorative finish that will last for years. As with the colour blue, shades of green tend to produce a refreshing feel, which is ideal for a larger bathroom.

IDEAS FOR A SCHEME

- Colours: in smaller rooms, lighter colours provide a greater feeling of space; darker shades can be used to highlight detailed areas, such as shelves and window frames.
- Renovating or redecorating: if you are having an entirely new bathroom, it is worth taking a little extra time to ensure that the decoration harmonizes with the fittings – it will be dependent on the colour of these fittings. Any wall colour will complement new white fittings, but if you choose strong colours for baths and basins, coordinating the scheme will be more difficult and future redecoration choices more limited.
- Attention to detail: bathrooms tend to be small, which means that all surfaces are close to the eye and prone to close scrutiny. Also, the very fact that people lounge in the bath gives plenty of opportunity for inspecting the decoration, and means that particular attention must be paid to all details in the room. It makes surface preparation that much more important, and the overall finishing requires extra care in order to produce the best possible result.
- Comfort: when choosing colours or textures, remember that the bathroom is an area where you want to be able to relax. An awareness of the effects of colour is important. Strong colours can be used, but bear in mind that they may not be restful. It really depends on your own personal preference and what sort of atmosphere and effect you want the decoration to create.

WHAT TO USE WHERE

S ome bathrooms are more suited to particular materials than others and, more importantly, specific areas in the room are better suited to one finish than another. You need to understand the particular properties of the various materials in order to use them in the right place and to the best effect.

TILES

Tiles are ideal for nearly all bathroom surfaces, but it is worth considering their size and shape, as well as the colour and finish, to determine what is going to be most suitable for your requirements.

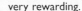

TILES IN THE BATHROOM

- Finish: it is best to use glazed rather than unglazed tiles, as the former are much easier to keep clean and, therefore, more hard-wearing.
- Size: although large tiles cover areas more quickly, they will show up any undulations or defects in wall surfaces much more readily. Also, a particularly small room is not ideal for large tiles as a lot of fiddly cuts are required, accuracy becomes more tricky and fitting large tiles into awkward areas can be very difficult.
- Showers and baths: tiles are the most commonly used decorating material around baths and in showers because of their water-repellent properties. However, these excellent properties only apply if grouting and sealing are carried out properly – tiling is not complete until the surface is totally waterproof.
- Using the range: tiles are available in all sizes, shapes and colours, such as border tiles, mosaics and tiled scenes. Surfaces need not be bland or repetitive, you can be as extravagant as you like – combining different colours, patterns and texture in your own individual style can be very rewarding.

PAINT

Paint is the most readily available of all decorating materials and is very easy to use. However, it is important to use the right paint in the right place, especially when painting a bathroom.

PAINT IN THE BATHROOM

- Hard-wearing: the most hard-wearing paints used to be oil- or solvent-based, but improved-formula, water-based equivalents are now nearly, if not totally, as good as their oil-based counterparts. Many manufacturers produce specific bathroom or moisture-resistant paints, which are ideal for bathroom surfaces. Otherwise, paints which contain vinyl are easily wipeable and ideal for bathroom use.
- Drying times: the other advantage of water-based paints is that they dry quickly, allowing for more than one coat to be applied in a day. Because the bathroom is such a busy area, this means that the job can be completed relatively quickly with little household upheaval.
  - Around baths and splashbacks: although this is normally the domain of tiles, these areas can be painted to good effect. Tongue-and-groove panelling looks particularly impressive around baths (see page 103). However, because of the constant water splashes, it is advisable to use an oil-based paint in these places (eggshell is ideal), making sure that the room is well ventilated during painting.

WALLPAPER IN THE BATHROOM

- Hard-wearing: use vinyl papers or, alternatively, varnish standard wallpapers after they have been applied.
- Avoiding damp: it is essential to keep paper away from areas prone to water splashes or excess moisture, such as splashbacks or the areas directly around baths. When first applied, wallpaper looks great, but in no time at all, the surface will deteriorate if it gets damp, whether it is vinyl-coated or protected with varnish.
- Extra adhesive: overlap adhesive can be used along the edges of all lengths of paper to ensure a better seal and make the paper less likely to lift.

WALLPAPER

There is no problem with using wallpaper in bathrooms as long as you follow the guidelines (see left) and use the correct type of paper.

PAINTING TECHNIQUES

A sound painting technique is the key to good finishing. It is important to use all decorating tools in the manner for which they were designed. Some tools can be used in a number of places, others are designed for specific areas. Before any painting can begin, though, surfaces must be prepared and an order of work drawn up.

COVERING UP

Surfaces that are not going to be painted must be covered up as overspray is difficult to remove, and serious spillages can result in ruined floor coverings. General purpose dust sheets are ideal for most surfaces, but tiles and fittings need extra care.

Masking tiles: paint roller overspray manages to find the smallest of areas to contaminate, such as the edges of tiles. Run some masking tape along the top edge of tiles to protect them before you start painting.

Masking fittings: bathroom fittings are particularly awkward shapes to cover. Lightweight plastic dust sheets are the best thing to use. Secure them with masking tape to keep them in place while painting is in progress.

PREPARING SURFACES

Thorough preparation of the surface is required before any decorating can take place – this is the process that makes the big difference between an average finish and an exceptional one.
- Wall surfaces: strip old wallpaper, fill holes and sand to a smooth finish. On particularly dusty surfaces, apply a coat of PVA solution (one part PVA to four parts water) to seal the walls before decorating.

- Wood: fill and sand as required.
- Washing down: wash down all the surfaces with a mild detergent, rinse and allow to dry before painting.
- Primers: on bare wood, use a good quality primer before applying the undercoat and top coats. On unpainted plaster, prime the surface for further coats by diluting the first coat of paint by one part water to 10 parts paint.

CHOOSING A TECHNIQUE

There are advantages and disadvantages with all the different methods of painting (see below). Choose the technique that suits you best and is the most appropriate for the conditions in your bathroom.

BRUSHES	The most multi-purpose of all painting tools. Ideal for all areas because of the different sizes available. Pure bristle brushes are still the best quality, although some synthetic fibre brushes are excellent for water-based paints.
ROLLERS	Make fast work of large open areas, but a brush will still be required to cut in around wall and ceiling edges. Choose the coarseness of the roller sleeve according to the finish required and the condition of the walls. Mohair rollers produce an exceptionally smooth finish.
PAINT PADS	Have the covering capability of rollers, are easy to use and economic on paint usage. Small pads can be used around edges, although a brush is often a better option.
PAINT SPRAYERS	Ideal for covering large areas quickly, but you need to mask off all the places that must be kept free of paint. Because of the fiddly nature of bathrooms and the lack of space, they are not ideally suited to this area of the home. Also, breathing apparatus is normally required when using paint sprayers.

CAUTION

When using paint, always make sure that the area is well ventilated – this is particularly important in a small bathroom. Leave windows and doors open to ensure a good through draught of air. Bathrooms often have slippery surfaces, so take extra care as dust sheets can slip on floors. Keep children and pets well out of the way while painting is in progress.

TILING TECHNIQUES

I t is almost certain that at some stage you will need to apply tiles to a bathroom wall. Understanding the basics of tiling is essential if you want to achieve a good finish: the secret is sound preparation, starting at the correct point, and ensuring the tiles are applied securely.

PREPARING SURFACES

Different surfaces need different preparation before tiles can be applied. The tile application will be more difficult and less effective if the surface is not properly prepared.

NEW PLASTER	Always seal new plaster with a PVA solution diluted four parts water to one part PVA. This stops the adhesive drying out too quickly when it is applied to the wall – which can turn tiling into a rushed job.
OLD PLASTER	As long as old plaster is sound, tiles can be applied directly to it. Fill any large holes with one-coat plaster; smaller areas can be filled with an all-purpose filler.
DRY-LINED	Dry-lined walls must be sealed with a PVA solution in the same way as new plaster to prevent adhesive drying out too quickly.
OLD TILES	As long as old tiles are securely attached to the wall surface, there is no reason why new tiles may not be applied directly over the top of them. Make sure that the old tiles are cleaned and sanded to give their surface a key for accepting adhesive. Any loose tiles should be removed and their spaces filled with patch plaster. However, if the tiled surface has a number of loose or broken tiles, it is best to start afresh by removing all the tiles with a cold chisel and hammer. Wear goggles to protect your eyes from flying debris.
WALLPAPER	Wallpaper must be removed from the walls before tiling them – use a steam stripper to speed up the process. Once all the paper is removed, fill holes, as necessary, then sand and, finally, seal the surface with a PVA solution.

ORDER OF WORK

Bathroom layouts vary, but there are certain guidelines that apply to nearly all rooms in order to achieve the best tiling results.

Follow the order of work so that Area 1 is finished before Area 2, and so on. Within each area, start at the bottom and work up.

Finish the main design before applying border tiles.

Finish with full tiles around the top.

If possible, have full tiles along the edge of the bath and take all other measurements from this point.

Join in corner with two half tiles, if necessary.

Attach a horizontal batten to the wall to give support for Area 1 to be tiled. Remove the batten once the tile adhesive has dried, in order to tile Area 5.

TECHNIQUE GUIDE

- Use wooden battens nailed level into walls as starting supports for the first rows of tiles. It is rare that the top of skirting boards are precisely level, and centralizing tile layouts often means that half tiles are required at the bottom of walls and the batten supports the first rows.
- Keep all the tile surfaces as flush as possible; reduce the adhesive on the back of any tiles that stick out

from the wall, and add some extra adhesive to any tiles that appear to have sunk.
- Keep some clean water and a sponge handy at all times, so that the excess adhesive can be cleaned off tile surfaces before it has a chance to dry.
- Buy a good quality tile cutter to deal with straight cuts, and a tile saw for dealing with curves and cutting holes for pipes.

HALF-TILING A BATHROOM

H alf-tiling a room offers the opportunity to combine tiled finishes with paper and/or paint to create a blend of different surfaces. Such a project involves all the basic tiling techniques and demonstrates the approach and order of work necessary for most tiling jobs.

1 Nail a horizontal supporting batten above the skirting board, making sure it is level. The gap left between this first row of tiles and the skirting board should be the size of half a tile. Avoid leaving a gap that will require small slithers as these are difficult to cut. Nail a vertical batten close to the corner to make a firm edge to butt the tiles up against. Apply adhesive to an area of about 1 sq m (1 sq yd) and fix the tiles in position on the wall. Use tile spacers to maintain gaps between the tiles.

3 Apply adhesive to the back of the cut tiles and position them along the corner junction. Make sure that the cut edge of each tile is positioned next to the corner, and use spacers to maintain even gaps between the tiles.

2 When the main wall surface has been tiled, remove the vertical batten and fill in along the corner junction with cut tiles. Mark off the cut required on each tile with a felt-tip pen, then use a tile cutter to score a line along the surface of the tile at the marked position. Once scored, move the tile up to between the bracket above the cutting wheel and below the sliding rails, positioning the scored line directly between the rails. Push down with even pressure to break the tile along the line.

4 Once the walls are covered with the main body of tiles to the required level, border tiles can be applied around the top edge of the tiles. Apply a generous amount of adhesive to the back of border tiles with a scraper then position them.

5 Relief border tiles, as shown here, require mitred joints in the corners in order to produce the best possible finish. Make the appropriate measurement, place the tile in a mitre block and then cut through it at the desired position with a tile saw.

6 Position the mitred tile in the corner and then continue with border tiles along the adjacent wall. Once the border is complete allow the adhesive to dry before grouting. When the grout has dried, polish the entire tiled surface with a dry cotton cloth.

BORDER TILE FRAME
Half-tiled rooms produce an attractive finish, with border tiles acting as the frame to the main body of tiles. A simple colour combination produces a very restful atmosphere.

PAINTING TILES

Tiles can be given an alternative finish by painting them. The finish of painted tiles will not be as hard-wearing as the normal glazed surface but, as long as the painted tiles are not under constant water attack, they can have a good life expectancy.

PRIMING THE TILES

Changing the entire surface colour of tiles requires thorough preparation to ensure that the paint adheres to the tiled surface. Before beginning, make sure that any gaps in the grout are filled and any broken tiles are replaced.

1 Clean the tiled surface with a mild detergent solution and then rinse with clean water. Allow the whole surface to dry.

2 Rub down the surface with silicone carbide paper. This scratches the glazed surface of the tiles and provides a key for the paint. Once sanded, wipe down the area again with a damp sponge to remove any dusty residue. Allow the surface to dry.

3 Paint the entire tile surface with proprietary tile primer and leave it to dry. This paint is specially formulated to provide a sound base for the application of coats of finishing paint.

CREATING A DESIGN

Most types of paint can be used to produce the desired colour or finish, as long as they are sealed with varnish after they have been applied. As an alternative to one solid colour, any number of different tile patterns can be created – the chequer-board design below is one simple, yet effective example.

Painting a chequer-board: paint the entire primed surface with white emulsion then paint alternate tiles with black emulsion. A fitch is the ideal size brush to produce neat straight lines. Allow the paint to dry then varnish the whole tiled surface to protect the finish.

USING CERAMICS

For the more adventurous decorator, small hand-painted designs can be applied to tiles with ceramic paint. Again, this finish should only be used in areas that are not under regular attack from water.

1 Trace a design from a book using a pencil. Stick the image to a tile with masking tape, making sure that it is centrally positioned on the tile and the pencilled side of the tracing paper is against the tile surface. Scribble over the design to transfer the pencil image onto the tile.

2 Remove the tracing paper and carefully fill in the design, using ceramic paints. Allow the paint to dry then varnish the whole of the tile surface to protect the design.

TRANSFERS AND STENCILS

Transfers and stencils are excellent decorations for transforming the look of tiles, especially when an old surface needs reviving, rather than totally replacing. Although transfers give a less hard-wearing surface than the normal glazed tiles, they are becoming more durable and are, therefore, perfectly acceptable to use on tiles.

APPLYING TRANSFERS

Transfers are fairly delicate and they require a great deal of care when moving them from their backing paper onto the tile. Manufacturers' guidelines vary, but this method is typical of the procedure recommended for most types.

1 Clean the tile that is going to have the transfer applied to it with a mild detergent and then rinse with clean water. Allow it to dry.

2 Soak the transfer (on its backing paper) in warm water for about 20 seconds then apply directly to the tile, as close to the required position as possible. The transfer should slide off the backing paper smoothly – the dampness of the area allows for final positioning of it before evaporation secures the image in place.

3 Using a dry cloth, very carefully dab the surface of the transfer to remove any small air bubbles and excess moisture.

STENCILLING TILES

Most paints can be used to stencil on tiles – it is the method of protecting the finish that is the secret of making sure that a stencilled image is long-lasting. Tiles can be primed first (see page 42), but it is not essential for such detailed painted areas. Make sure the tiles are cleaned and allowed to dry thoroughly before applying the stencil.

1 Stick the stencil securely in position on the tile surface using masking tape.

2 Apply paint with a stencil brush, using short dabbing motions and keeping the angle of the bristles as perpendicular as possible to the tiled surface. Remove the excess paint from the brush before applying it, otherwise the paint may seep under the edges of the stencil and distort the finished picture.

3 Remove the stencil carefully and allow the paint to dry completely. Meanwhile, wash the stencil and dry it thoroughly. Tape the stencil directly over the dried painted image on the tile and apply some ceramic varnish, using the stencil brush. Make sure that all areas of the image are covered. Remove the stencil and allow the varnish to dry, producing a well-protected stencil image.

APPLYING WALLPAPER

The method of applying wallpaper in a bathroom is the same as in any other room in the house, but there are special precautions you can take to make sure that the paper lasts as long as possible, and can cope with moist air and the problems associated with it. Vinyl papers are the best option, although other papers can be used.

BEFORE TILING

A complete bathroom makeover provides the opportunity to wallpaper before any tiles are applied. Although this is not the essential order of work, it does help to guarantee a long-lasting wallpaper finish.

1 Draw an accurate pencil guideline to show where the final row of tiles will be positioned on the wall. Apply the wallpaper so that the bottom edge comes approximately 12 mm (½ in) below the pencil line.

2 When the wallpapering is complete and the tiles are applied, the top row of tiles will cover this bottom edge of the paper and prevent it from lifting when the bathroom is damp and steamy.

STRENGTHENING THE PASTE

- Pastable papers: if using wallpapers that require pasting before application, make the paste mix slightly stronger than the manufacturer's recommendations for that type of paper. This makes a firmer bond with the wall and extends the life of the wallpaper.
- Ready-pasted papers: the soaking and application process is normally enough to secure these wallpapers on walls in most rooms; however, for a bathroom it may be worth 'double pasting' them. Although ready-pasted paper comes with paste applied to it, treat it as though it is unpasted. Don't soak it in water, but apply a coat of normal wallpaper paste and leave it to soak in before applying the paper to the wall.

PRODUCING A PROFESSIONAL FINISH

In addition to all the normal rules of wallpaper application, there are one or two extra procedures that can be carried out in bathrooms to give a totally professional finish. Follow the manufacturer's recommendations and make sure that the wallpaper has soaked for the appropriate time before applying it. Have all the wallpapering tools to hand before you start. Keep areas as clean as possible at all times and, above all, make sure that from the very first sheet the pattern is correctly joined and that the paper is vertical.

Corners: apply the paper in the usual way then peel back corner overlaps before they dry and apply some overlap or border adhesive along the entire corner junction before securing it back in place. This creates a doubly strong bond. Remove excess adhesive with a damp sponge.

Varnishing: non-vinyl papers can be varnished to give a protective coat to their finish. Some vinyl papers will accept varnish, but it is best to try a small test area first.

Windows: bathroom window reveals are very prone to condensation, which will quickly lift paper edges if not treated. Run a bead of silicone along the frame/paper junction to prevent any paper from lifting.

Skirting boards: apply a bead of decorator's caulk along the junction of skirting and paper, allow it to dry, then paint the skirting as normal. The caulk provides an extra seal and prevents paper edges from lifting.

PAINT EFFECTS

C reating a good paint effect has as much to do with having the correct glaze mixture as the actual application. Nowadays, acrylic ready-mixed glazes are widely available; once mixed with colourizers, they are easy to apply and create stunning paint effects. Acrylic glaze is best applied over a water-based paint base coat – vinyl silk emulsion provides the longest 'working' time for the glaze on the wall.

COLOURWASHING

Colourwashing is one of the simplest effects to produce, giving an excellent finish that creates depth and texture on the wall surface. It is ideal on slightly rough plastered walls as it highlights this rustic feature and gives the room a relaxing, comfortable atmosphere.

1 Apply the glaze in all directions across the wall surface using a normal paint brush. Work in areas of approximately 1 sq m (1 sq yd) so that the glaze does not dry out too quickly.

2 Rub a clean, slightly dampened cotton rag over the wall to remove the excess glaze, leaving the remnants to highlight any slight depressions in the painted surface. Rub off as little or as much of the glaze as you like, depending on the amount of colour you want to leave on the wall.

CREATING ATMOSPHERE
Simple, yet very effective, colourwashing produces a great impact with relatively little skill required.

RAG-ROLLING

Standard paint effects can be combined with other techniques to produce a more individual look in your bathroom. It can be very fulfilling trying out complex effects like rag-rolling in the bathroom because the wall spaces are generally smaller than in other areas of the home and you can see the results of your efforts really quickly.

I

2

I Apply a base coat to the wall and allow it to dry. Draw a number of equidistant, vertical lines across the surface, making very light pencil marks. Run masking tape along each line edge to produce a masked-off, striped effect.

2 Have a number of rolled-up dampened rags to hand before applying the glaze to two or three of the areas between the masking tape. Do not apply glaze to all the masked-off areas at once as the glaze will dry before you can rag-roll all of it.

3 Form a damp rag into a sausage shape and roll it down the wall through a glazed area. Change to a different rag for each stripe and rinse the rags between each new glaze application. Repeat the process until all the stripes are done then remove the masking tape.

3

STRIPED EFFECT
Combining the austere, straight lines of stripes with a rag-rolled effect produces a wonderfully clean and refreshing look on a wall.

COMBINING PAINT EFFECTS

S ome paint effects complement each other very well and can be used together on a single surface. Many of these effects use specific tools, which you will need to practise using before you can achieve the best results. It is worth building up a paint-effect toolkit, so that you can experiment with effects and produce finishes of your own design.

COMBING AND DRAGGING

Combing and dragging combine well as both have a pronounced texture that creates a very definite pattern on the wall surface. Both are suited to small areas – they can be overwhelming on large open surfaces. The panelled design shown here is an excellent compromise, reducing the amount of wall coverage of each effect while still producing a finish of considerable impact.

1

2

1 Mask off some equal-sized panels on the wall, using floor tiles as a template. Measure a second panel inside the first, and mask off along its edges before glazing inside the panel with an ordinary paintbrush.

2 Starting at the top left-hand corner of the panel, make vertical sweeps down through the glaze using a graining comb.

3 After every second or third sweep with the comb, wipe the excess glaze from the comb with a dry cotton cloth. Once the vertical sweeps have been completed, use the same technique to create horizontal sweeps across the entire panel.

3

4 Allow the glaze to dry, remove the masking tape, and apply more tape around the outside of the outer panel. Although it would be easier to mask off the internal combed panel, the tape can pull away the glazed surface when removed and a glazed surface can be difficult to touch-in. Apply glaze to the outer 'frame', taking care not to get any on the internal combed area.

5 Use a fairly coarse-bristled brush to drag through the glaze along each side of the 'frame'. A dragging brush could be used, but they are generally much wider than the area allows. Angle the brush so that it is at a very acute angle to the wall surface and make smooth, even sweeps in the glaze.

6 Make sure you create a definite 'square' join between each side of the frame, as precise finishing at corners adds to the effect. When the frame is complete, remove the masking tape. Continue with other panels, repeating steps 1-6.

TEXTURED PANELLING
This panelled effect is impressive in any room, but in a bathroom the matching shapes of the tiles and the panels produces a very smart and well-integrated decorative scheme.

PAINTED SCENES

H and-painted scenes and expansive murals are difficult projects because they require considerable artistic talent. However, it is possible for anybody to use stencils and stamps to produce designs for small localized wall areas or as part of a big picture.

STENCILS

DIY outlets and craft shops sell stencils to suit all tastes, but it can be very rewarding to make your own unique stencils. All you have to do is draw or trace a simple design, transfer it to a piece of acetate, then carefully cut out the design to produce your own custom-made stencil.

1 Lay a sheet of acetate on top of the drawn or traced design and then use a felt-tip pen to transfer the design onto the acetate surface.

2 Place the acetate on a cutting mat or use an old offcut of building board. Using a craft knife, cut out the required sections of the design.

STENCILLING

- Paint the design with rhythmic dabbing motions of the brush.
- As well as custom-made brushes, other tools can be used for stencilling designs, such as paint crayons and aerosol paints.
- Create depth by applying more paint to the outer edges of a stencil design – this produces a more three-dimensional effect. Building up colour on one side of the design produces a shadow.

3 Secure the stencil with masking tape then paint the design. Remove excess paint from the brush before each application and keep it perpendicular to the wall surface.

STAMPING

Stamps are an easy way of applying specific images to a wall surface. These can be home-made, but the process is very time consuming, especially when creating anything more than a simple, straightforward design. The growing popularity of stamping means that you can now buy a wide range of designs.

1 Spread paint evenly on the stamp with a brush or a custom-made foam roller. Apply the stamp to the wall surface, pressing down firmly to make sure all areas of the stamp are in full contact with the wall.

2 Lift the stamp carefully to avoid it sliding across the wall surface and smudging the paint. Vary the intensity of the image according to your personal taste by adjusting the amount of paint applied to the stamp and by removing excess paint from the stamp before applying it to the wall surface.

COMBINING EFFECTS

Stamps and stencils are ideal paint effects to combine on a wall, as each brings its own character to a painted scene. They can be used to make a variety of different scenes for the bathroom. Ocean motifs are popular.

MULTI-COLOURED EFFECTS
The single colour of stamps, mixed with the more broken, multi-coloured effect of stencils, creates a wonderful combination of colour and design on this bathroom wall.

PROTECTING WORK

T he life expectancy of paint and wallpaper in the bathroom will always be less than in other areas of the home, but by carrying out a few extra tasks, this period can be lengthened considerably.

Dealing with moist air: the most significant damage done to bathroom surfaces results from lingering moist air and condensation. Fitting an effective extractor fan in a bathroom is, therefore, the single most important task to carry out. Unfortunately, in most cases, it is not a particularly straightforward task and it is worth seeking professional advice for both positioning and fitting.

Polishing tiles: to prolong the life of tile grout, clean the tiled surfaces from time to time with a silicone-based polish. This gives the grout an extra seal to protect it and maintain its colour.

Sealing effects: the glaze used for paint effects doesn't provide the most hard-wearing of finishes and the surface requires further protection, especially in a bathroom. Use a matt varnish or proprietary emulsion glaze coat on all paint effects. This will also give a surface that can be wiped easily.

Renovating Floors

RENOVATING FLOORS

Bathroom flooring is largely a matter of personal choice – whether you prefer the warm feel of carpet underfoot, or the water-repellent properties of hard tiles and vinyl. Most types of floor covering are suitable and, like any other decorative system, they have both advantages and disadvantages. However, the one consistent factor, which remains the same for any bathroom flooring, is its hard-wearing quality – this must be considered thoroughly before making a final decision. This chapter explains the pros and cons of the different types of floor covering and illustrates the best way of laying them.

CHOOSING A STYLE

The floor style of your bathroom will almost certainly be directly affected by the decoration of the room – the paint, paper and tiles will all influence the final decision. Cost is also a relevant factor: although carpeting a floor may be cheaper than laying tiles, the carpet will need replacing more quickly. Also, in small bathrooms it may be possible to use vinyl offcuts from other areas of the house, such as the kitchen. Alternatively, simply painting the floor can produce a great effect at a relatively low cost.

Keeping the wooden look: original wooden floors, or newly laid planking, provide a very natural, simplistic floor covering that is relatively hard-wearing as well as decorative. Such floors must be treated with the appropriate varnish or a coat of proprietary sealant to protect them from water attack.

The softer approach: carpets or natural floor coverings, such as coir and seagrass, give a much more cushioned feel underfoot than the harder alternatives. Using the same floor covering in adjoining rooms gives a feeling of continuity and links the decoration as a whole.

Tiling floors: solid and hard-wearing, tiles produce an excellent finish in most bathrooms. It is essential that the correct technique is used when laying tiles, as mistakes can prove costly. Try and choose a design, whether extravagant or simple, that complements the surrounding decoration and gives a harmonious feel to the overall scheme.

Using paint: the easiest option can often be the most effective. Older floorboards, especially, benefit from a well-chosen paint colour; as the floor ages and distresses, the overall look often improves. Proprietary floor paint is the professional choice, but less hard-wearing paints can be used if a gradually ageing and naturally distressed look is required.

RESTORING FLOORBOARDS

R estoring a planked floor to its former glory is a fairly arduous task, but the rewards are very worthwhile. Before old floorboards can be recoated with varnish, all old and ingrained coatings must be removed. For a small floor area, you can hire a sander to do this.

1 Use a hammer and punch to knock in any protruding nail heads on the floor before beginning to sand. Failure to do this will damage the sander.

2 Edging sanders have orbital sanding heads that rotate and vibrate at the same time. Always follow the manufacturer's guidelines for use. Run the sander up and down the floor surface, working with the grain. On the first sweeps with the sander, use rough abrasive paper then gradually work down to smoother grades. The whole floor should be sanded three or four times, progressively reducing the coarseness of the abrasive paper.

3 When the whole floor is sanded, vacuum up the sawdust and clean away the remnants with a cloth dampened in white spirit. As soon as the white spirit has evaporated, the floor is ready to finish with varnish or sealant.

LARGE FLOORS

For larger bathrooms, you need to hire a drum sander as well as an edger. The technique of reducing the abrasive paper coarseness is used (see opposite), but a slightly more methodical order of work is required to produce an evenly sanded surface. Follow the manufacturer's guidelines for use and always wear a dust mask. Always tilt the sander back before starting it, otherwise you may damage the floorboards while the sander is stationary but turned on.

First, sand at 45 degrees to the line of the floorboards.

Next, sand at 45 degrees in the opposite direction.

Finally, sand with the grain of the boards.

Use overlapping sweeps with the sander.

Finish around the perimeter of the room with an edging sander.

HARDBOARDING A FLOOR

Hardboarding is a method of floor preparation that is used to cover floorboards before laying vinyl coverings, or where floorboards are old and uneven and a flat surface is required for laying carpet. Before hardboarding, make sure that any access to underfloor surfaces is not going to be covered over – install inspection hatches in the hardboard, if necessary.

1 Ensure that all floorboards are secure, screwing down any creaky boards before you cover them with hardboard. Do not use screws that extend below floor level because they may pierce underfloor wires or pipes.

2 Secure the hardboard in position, shiny side up, using a hammer and hardboarding nails or a custom-made staple gun. Small sheets of hardboard measuring 1 m 20 cm x 60 cm (4 x 2 ft) are the ideal size for bathrooms, as they are easy to manoeuvre. Stagger the edges of the hardboard sheets, so that no run of joins extends in a single line across the room. Secure the sheets every 15 cm (6 in) in all directions.

3 To cut hardboard sheets to fit smaller areas, use a craft knife and a straight edge, such as a spirit level, to score the hardboard (see below). Turn the sheet over and snap the cut area upwards so the sheet breaks along the scored line. It can then be fitted as normal.

CAUTION

Remember never to position your supporting hand in front of the craft-knife blade when you are cutting the hardboard.

4 Use a paper template to cut around awkward areas. Cut slits in a sheet of paper then mould it around the base of an obstruction, such as a basin pedestal. Crease the slits into the profile of the pedestal and mark along the fold in the slits with a pencil.

5 Remove the paper, straighten out the slits, and cut along the pencil guideline to reveal the exact profile of the pedestal. Place the template on some hardboard and draw around it with the pencil to show the line around which you have to cut.

6 For cutting curves in hardboard, use a jigsaw rather than a craft knife. Follow the manufacturer's guidelines on how to use the saw and do not ignore their safety instructions.

7 Test the cut hardboard for size around the obstacle. Fix it in place using hardboarding nails or a staple gun. Use nails that are not long enough to pierce under-floor pipes.

DECORATING FLOORBOARDS

There are any number of different colour and design possibilities for prepared floors: they can be given a traditional waxed, or varnished finish or they can be painted or stained with equal effectiveness. It is possible to produce all kinds of unusual finishes by experimenting with coloured stains and various paint effects, tailoring them to the needs of the room.

SIMPLE STAINING AND VARNISHING

Changing the natural wood colour with stain and varnish is an easy way of altering the look of traditional floorboards. It is a relatively simple procedure as long as you follow the application guidelines below.

Keeping to edges: treat each of the floorboards as a separate item when applying a stain. Try not to overlap the stain as this can lead to a very patchy finish that shows up brush marks rather than the natural grain of the wood. Work steadily across the floor, ensuring that a wet edge is constantly maintained between application strokes.

Going two-tone: a very effective decorative option for staining is to use two different colours and stain alternate floorboards. You can choose similar colours or a more definite contrast, as shown here. The technique of treating floorboards as separate items is clearly even more important in this case.

Protecting the finish: whatever the decorative finish, the floorboards must be varnished to protect them. Use a water-based varnish so that more than one coat can be applied in a day, and the bathroom can be back in use as soon as possible. Brush the varnish over the floorboards, taking care to cover the whole area so the entire floor is protected.

FLOOR DISTRESSING

There are a number of ways of giving a distressed look to floorboards. One of the quickest and easiest is the technique demonstrated here, which uses two water-based emulsion paint colours to add interest to the finish. For the best result, make the second colour darker than the first. Between the coats of paint, masking fluid is applied to random areas. This prevents the top coat of paint from adhering properly and allows the bottom coat to show through. The overall effect is a colourful, distressed look.

1 Apply a base coat of emulsion directly onto the floorboards, working the paint into all areas. Allow it to dry.

2 Apply small, random streaks of masking fluid across the floor surface, paying particular attention to floorboard edges.

3 Paint a second colour, preferably a darker colour, across the entire floor surface. Allow it to dry before sanding the surface.

4 Sand the floor surface with fine grade abrasive paper. In the areas that had masking fluid applied to them the bottom coat will show through. The floor can be varnished to protect it or it can be allowed to distress further with general day-to-day wear and tear.

TILING THE FLOOR

Hard tiles are the most hard-wearing of all bathroom floor options, but they require some planning and preparation before they can be applied. They cannot be laid directly on floorboards so sheets of 18 mm (¾ in) ply should be laid and fixed on the floorboards to act as a base on which they can be placed. Once a secure base is established, it is vital to plan the order of work and make sure that tiling is started in the correct place.

The bottom of the door may require shaving as the tiles and base board raise the floor level considerably.

Walls are rarely completely 'square' in a room, therefore the skirting can never be trusted as a straight guideline.

Position of first tile.

Start with the farthest full tiles from the door. Nail a batten into the floor to butt the first row of tiles up against.

Centre the design so that cuts are as evenly balanced as possible around the perimeter.

Full tiles – tile first.

Cut tiles – tile second.

Finish cut tiles once full tiles have dried. Start from farthest corner and work back to the door.

STARTING POINT

Rather than start in the corner of the room, position the first tile so that the distance to the walls either side is equidistant. This way any cut tiles will be next to the walls, keeping the full tile design in the centre of the room (see opposite page for the technique).

FLOOR TILING TECHNIQUE

Tiling a floor is a methodical process, that is relatively straightforward as long as the floor has been well prepared. Fix a wooden batten to support the first row of tiles. It is best to use a flexible adhesive to deal with any slight floor movement when tiling on a suspended floor. Keep a constant check that tiles are laid level and gaps between tiles are kept consistent with tile spacers. Tiles can be cut with a standard tile cutter, which is normally strong enough to deal with most floor tiles. An electric tile cutter can be hired for particularly thick floor tiles, or for tiles that require a lot of detailed cutting in order to go around awkward shapes or other obstacles in the bathroom.

1 Apply adhesive to the floor and lay the first tile tight against the supporting batten.

2 Cut tiles as necessary, using a standard tile cutter or an electric tile cutter. If hiring a cutter, follow the manufacturer's instructions for use and safety.

3 Apply adhesive directly to the back of the cut tiles and fix them in position. Allow to dry.

4 Finish the surface with grout specifically designed for floor tiles. Use a grout spreader to press the grout into all tile joints. Remove excess grout from the tile surfaces before it dries, using a damp sponge.

LAYING VINYL

V inyl bridges the gap between hard-tile floors and carpets. Hard-
wearing and water-repellent, it makes an ideal bathroom flooring,
which, although slightly cold underfoot, has a more cushioned feel
than hard tiles but is not as soft as carpet. Sheet vinyl is tricky to fit,
so take the time to measure and cut carefully to avoid mistakes.

MAKING A TEMPLATE

To get a roll of vinyl into a manageable size to fit in the bathroom, you need
to make a template of the bathroom floor and transfer it onto the vinyl. This
makes the trimming and fitting process much easier and also allows for the
approximate positioning of the vinyl before it is finally fitted in place.

Use sheets of newspaper and
masking tape to make an exact
template of the bathroom
floor.

Cut precisely around the
pedestal edges.

Place template on unrolled
vinyl and cut around edge,
adding 5 cm (2 in) onto the
template size to allow for final
fitting when positioned in the
bathroom.

FITTING GUIDELINES

Vinyl is not a flexible floor covering because it will not stretch; therefore, accurate cutting is vital. Even the most experienced floor layers take extra time when laying vinyl, as it is very difficult to rectify mistakes once an incorrect cut has been made.

Straight lines: use a sharp craft knife to cut straight edges next to skirting boards. Crease the vinyl as firmly as possible into the floor/skirting junction to ensure an accurate cut.

Cutting curves: around curved areas such as toilet pedestals, cut small slits in the vinyl to help mould it around the pedestal profile then trim it with the craft knife. Vinyl does not have to be stuck down around the edge, but it is a good idea to use double-sided tape or proprietary vinyl adhesive.

Joining: in larger bathrooms it may be necessary to join sheets of vinyl. In these cases, always join two factory edges, and use double-sided tape to make sure that both pieces are stuck firmly to the floor.

Extra sealing: because of the moisture in bathrooms, it is a good idea to run a bead of silicone sealant around the perimeter of the vinyl to prevent water getting under the vinyl surface. To make a neat finish, mask the floor/skirting junction with two strips of masking tape, apply the silicone, then remove the tape immediately.

CARPETING FLOORS

C arpet provides the softest underfoot option for bathrooms, making it the most popular choice for many people. Carpets are easier to fit than vinyl, although many of the techniques used in fitting are similar. There are two main types available: foam-backed carpets and the generally better quality hessian-backed carpets. There are small differences in laying the carpets, depending on which type you are fitting. Making a template of the floor (see page 66) is a good way of cutting carpet roughly to size before fitting it.

FOAM-BACKED CARPETS

As the name suggests, foam-backed carpets are constructed so that the carpet fibres are joined directly onto a foam backing, which provides a cushioning layer designed to eliminate the need for underlay. These carpets tend to be less expensive, and easier to fit, than hessian-backed carpets. There is a large range of differing thicknesses and qualities available.

1 Position the carpet, trim it to size with a craft knife, then remove it. Run double-sided carpeting tape around the perimeter of the room.

2 Roll the carpet out slowly, pressing the edges firmly onto the tape to secure it in position on the floor.

SUB-FLOOR IMPROVEMENT

Although foam-backed carpet has a cushioned effect, the quality of the carpet being laid and the evenness of the floor will determine how good that effect is. Rough floorboards or an uneven floor provide a poor base for carpet unless you hardboard them first (see pages 60-61). Another simple way of improving the sub-floor is to put down layers of newspaper as underlay.

HESSIAN-BACKED CARPETS

Fitting hessian-backed carpets is a slightly lengthier process and involves the fitting of gripper rods to hold the carpet in place. Underlay is also required under the carpet to provide a cushioned feel underfoot. Underlay is supplied in rolls about 90 cm (3 ft) in width. It can be rolled directly onto the floor surface, trimmed to fit, and then the carpet can be laid over the top.

1 Fit gripper rods all the way around the perimeter of the floor. Make sure there is a small gap of 5 mm (⅕ in) between the rods and the skirting board. Hold a hardboard offcut next to the skirting board to avoid scuffing it with the hammer when nailing the rods in place.

2 Cut some gripper rods into small sections to go around any curved edges such as the toilet pedestal. Once all the gripper rods have been fitted, roll out the underlay across the entire floor, making sure that it is fitted to the edge of the gripper rods, but not over them.

3 Lay out the roughly fitted carpet, creasing it into the floor/skirting junction. Cut to fit over the gripper rods to the wall, using a sharp craft knife. Use a carpet stretcher to flatten out the carpet surface, placing it under slight tension as it binds around the edges with the gripper rods.

4 Use a bolster chisel to push the edge of the carpet over and behind the gripper rods to secure it firmly in position.

FLOOR COVERING CHECKLIST

I t can be useful to weigh up all the pros and cons of the different floor covering options before making a final decision about your bathroom floor. As well as taking into account the flooring techniques shown in this chapter, the good and bad points of the various floorings themselves will affect your decision.

PROS AND CONS OF BATHROOM FLOORING

FLOOR TYPE	Durability	Ease of cleaning	Preparation	Laying/ Finishing	Expense
	poor ✔ excellent ✔✔✔✔✔	difficult ✔ easy ✔✔✔✔✔	lengthy ✔ quick ✔✔✔✔✔	difficult ✔ easy ✔✔✔✔✔	high cost ✔ low cost ✔✔✔✔✔
Hessian-backed carpet	✔✔✔	✔✔✔	✔✔	✔✔✔	✔✔
Foam-backed carpet	✔✔	✔✔✔	✔✔✔	✔✔✔✔	✔✔✔✔
Vinyl	✔✔✔✔	✔✔✔✔✔	✔✔	✔	✔✔
Stripped flooring	✔✔✔✔	✔✔✔	✔✔✔	✔✔✔✔✔	✔✔✔✔✔
Painted flooring	✔✔✔	✔✔	✔✔✔✔	✔✔✔✔✔	✔✔✔✔✔
Hard tile	✔✔✔✔✔	✔✔✔✔✔	✔	✔✔	✔

Fixtures and Fittings

FIXTURES AND FITTINGS

The wallpaper and paintwork are not the only things that give a bathroom its decorative appeal. The fixtures and fittings that make the room fully functional are just as important. Lighting, bath screens and window decorations are just a few of the areas that need to be integrated into the overall design scheme to produce the desired finish. The number of fittings will depend on both room size and personal requirements but, regardless of the number, fittings must be positioned correctly and secured in place as professionally as possible. Most of these fitting tasks can be carried out by a practical home decorator, although it may be necessary to seek professional help in some areas – if any electrical wiring is required, for example.

SHOWER AND BATH SCREENS

S hower and bath screens are used to prevent splashes of water from covering bathroom surfaces while someone is using the shower. A screen is required where a bath and shower are integrated – when they are separate, a shower is more likely to be housed in a cubicle made of several interlocking screens. Whichever type is suitable, most of the manufacturers supply adequate, although varied guidelines for fitting.

Bath screening: bath screens are quite straightforward to fit and those made of clear glass provide a relatively unobtrusive mechanism for containing a bath and integrated shower. Many consist of two main screens, one of which can slide out across the bath rim to extend the overall screen length and so prevent any overspray onto the bathroom floor when the shower is in operation.

4

Shower cubicles: separate showers are best housed in an enclosed cubicle to prevent water spraying over the floor. Any number of designs and screen shapes are available, but make sure that your chosen screen fits the shower-tray dimensions. Access to the shower can be by means of a customized (watertight) hinged door, or a sliding door similar to the mechanism on bath screens.

FITTING AFTER TILING

If possible, fit a bath screen before tiling the bathroom; if fitting after tiling, you will need to use a tile drill bit to make holes in the tiles for the screen fixings.

FITTING A BATH SCREEN

As the function of a bath screen is to create a watertight barrier, this must be the primary consideration when fitting it – concentrate your efforts on keeping the screen completely vertical, easily operational, and fitted in the correct position according to the shower requirements. Make sure that the base of the retaining bracket sits central to the bath rim so water will run down onto the rim and back into the bath when the screen is fitted.

1 Use a long spirit level to ensure that the bath screen's retaining bracket is positioned so that it is precisely vertical, and that the base sits central to the bath rim. Use a pencil to mark its position on the wall and also where the retaining screw holes should be drilled.

2 Remove the bracket and drill holes ready to house the retaining screws. Depending on the wall surface and the method of fixing, wall plugs may be required. If this is the case, insert them at this stage, making sure that drill-bit size, plug size and screw size all correspond.

3 Hold the bracket back in place, checking that it is vertical once more, and screw the bracket in position on the wall.

4 Fit the screen into the bracket following the manufacturer's guidelines. Apply some silicone around the wall/screen junction to provide a watertight seal.

MIRRORS

M irrors are seen as one of the more essential bathroom fittings, and it is rare to come across a bathroom that does not have at least one. As well as being practical, mirrors can also be used decoratively – achieving different effects within specific bathroom surroundings. Size, shape and style are all important considerations when fitting mirrors in your bathroom.

Creating space: mirrors are perfect for creating an impression of greater space in a small room and they are particularly well suited to bathrooms, especially if you can have a large wall area of mirrors to enhance this reflective effect.

Being practical: remember that the main function of most mirrors is a practical one, and this should be taken into account when positioning them. However, practicality can be married with decorative appeal to produce interesting effects.

Decorative priorities: where practicality is not the foremost concern, a mirror can be more of a decorative accessory – its style and position combining with other features in the room to enhance the overall decor. In certain cases, the period or style of the mirror can add to the authenticity of the room's decorative scheme.

USING SCREW FIXINGS

Mirrors can be hung like pictures on hooks; for a flatter finish against the wall, they can be screwed in flush against the wall with specially designed screws that hold the mirror in place while providing an attractive finish.

1 Drill holes in the wall for the number of screw fixings required. Fit wall plugs, if necessary, then fit small rubber grommets into the holes in the mirror to stop it cracking when the screws are tightened. Tighten the screws, without overtightening them.

2 Fit dome-shaped covers to the mirror screws – they have a threaded core that is designed so that these covers can be screwed into them. The covers hide the screw heads and provide a more aesthetically pleasing finish to the mirror.

USING ADHESIVE

Some mirrors are not made with factory-drilled holes for fixing. In this case, it is better to glue the mirror in position on the wall, using proprietary mirror adhesive. The mirror must be supported on a batten until the adhesive has set.

1 Nail a horizontal batten into the wall. Apply a generous amount of mirror adhesive to the back of the mirror – a wavy line pattern ensures good adhesion when the mirror is bedded in position on the wall.

2 Position the mirror, resting it on the batten. Do not remove the batten until the adhesive has totally dried, otherwise the mirror may slip or fall off the wall. Once dry, remove the batten and fill and sand the holes.

LIGHTING

L ight, whether natural or artificial, can have a profound effect on any bathroom scheme. It requires careful thought to decide what best suits the atmosphere of the room and its decoration, and fulfils the practical requirements of the room. For safety reasons, electrical work should be carried out by a qualified electrician.

Focusing light: downlighting can be aimed directly at a certain part of the room so that a specific task can be carried out. Experimenting with varying levels of light can produce different moods while retaining the directional function.

DIRECTIONAL LIGHTING

Everyday bathroom activities necessitate light sources that are directional and can be used to clearly light up certain areas. This function may be included in the overall lighting set-up in the room, but in many cases it can be confined to more direct-task lighting, designed to direct light exactly where you want it.

Even lighting: fluorescent strips give good overall lighting. They can be used close to basins and vanity units to provide excellent light consistency, and this effect can be exaggerated by the use of mirrors.

Downlighting: rather than aiming light at one particular part of the room, overall downlighting tends to give even light throughout the room, making all areas relatively consistent in terms of their light level.

Wall lighting: wall lights come in a large selection of styles and strengths. They give you the option of focusing light up or down, depending on personal requirements and mood preferences for the room.

Natural light: during daytime, natural light can produce a very invigorating and enlivening atmosphere. However, by the evening, this can change to a calmer feeling which can be enhanced by soft artificial light.

BATHROOM ACCESSORIES

B athroom accessories can transform the look of the room, so accessory style is an important design element. Whether the accessories are essential or optional, large or small, make sure that they blend with the room's decoration and add to its overall appeal.

TOWEL RAILS

Most bathrooms require something to hang towels on to dry, and heated towel rails are ideal for speeding up this process. The functional role of the towel rail can combine with the look of other accessories in the room – whether traditional, or more modern and innovative – to provide a well-integrated scheme.

Traditional rails: simple in construction and style, a traditional rail fits well into an established bathroom surrounding. Whether electrically powered, or part of the central heating system as shown here, a traditional rail is practical as well as smart.

Modern systems: in recent years, rail designs have become more varied and innovative. Using the heat from radiators to dry out items on a fixed framework of rails is a way of extending the function of the radiator, while producing an unusual alcove design that fits well into a modern bathroom design.

CHANGING FITTINGS

All the smaller bathroom fittings are quick and simple to change, making it easy to alter the appearance of wall surfaces. Bathroom makeovers do not have to be complex and time consuming to achieve a change in style.

Fitting the fittings: many essential wall fittings come supplied with a paper template that makes marking for drill fixings much easier. Simply position the template and mark the drilling points on the wall.

The simplest of changes: cord pulls for lights are often a neglected area of change. Many variations on the standard plastic theme are available and can be fitted in seconds.

DOOR LOCKS

Bathroom locking systems come in all manner of designs and sizes – it is really a matter of personal choice and what suits your bathroom. Locking systems that are separate from the handle mechanism are one option, although a fully integrated handle and locking system can often provide the neatest solution.

Operating the lock: integral systems work on a locking screw centrally positioned on the bathroom handle.

Child safety: the beauty of an integral system is that most can be opened from the outside with a special safety key. This means a trapped child can easily be freed with little fuss.

DECORATING BATHROOM ACCESSORIES

M ost bathroom accessories can be transformed with paint, varnish and all manner of other standard decorating materials, whether you are renovating older items or starting from new.

NEW TOILET SEATS

One of the last outposts of mundane practicality has at last been reached by the modern world of design and progress. The style, colour and finish of your toilet seat are now as important a part of bathroom makeovers as any other fitting. The natural wood look is one option for a seat; it is very easy to recoat with varnish, giving it excellent life expectancy as well as attractive looks.

Fitting seats: most seats are designed with universal fittings that slot into the retaining holes at the back of the toilet pan. These fittings can be adjusted to fit the size of most toilets, but it is always worth checking that this is the case with your chosen design before you buy it.

RENOVATING AN OLD SEAT

4

Old plastic seats have little character of their own, but a quick change of colour can integrate a seat into a specific bathroom scheme. Remove the seat before painting to protect the pan and allow access to all areas of the seat itself.

1 Plastic seats need to be cleaned thoroughly before painting, using a proprietary surface preparation solution. This should be wiped onto the seat and then polished off to remove all dirt.

2 Spray the seat with several coats of acrylic paint, keeping the aerosol about 15 cm (6 in) from the seat surface. Work in smooth sweeping movements, applying several thin coats rather than a few thick ones. Follow the manufacturer's guidelines on aerosol safety; at the very least, you will need to wear a respiratory mask.

2

BATHROOM CHAIRS

Room for furniture is often severely limited in bathrooms because of their size; however, there is often space for the odd item, such as a bathroom chair. These can be used as a movable decorative item, which can either complement the surrounding decoration or provide a contrast. Aerosol paint effects, such as crackle glaze, are ideal for painting awkwardly shaped items.

1 Sand down the chair surface, and use a damp cloth to wipe off any dusty residue. Holding the aerosol about 15 cm (6 in) from the chair surface, work across the chair. Turn the chair round and then over to get to all the less accessible areas.

2 Allow the chair to dry and the crackle effect to develop. When it is dry, spray the entire chair with a protective aerosol varnish.

THE AGED EFFECT
The crackle glaze on this chair provides a wonderfully aged look, which would look good in almost any bathroom scheme.

WINDOW SHUTTERS

W indows can be a problem area when decorating bathrooms as the choice of window dressings is frequently limited by the amount of available space. There may not be enough room for curtains, so producing a finish that ties in with the rest of the decoration can be difficult. Window shutters are an attractive option as they do not take up much room and can be very effective when limited to half the overall window size, in a café-curtain style.

1 Measure the exact width and height of the window reveal to establish the required dimensions of the shutters.

2 Make the two doors out of fretwork panelling by cutting the panel to the exact size of the doors, allowing in the measurements for two lengths of 5 x 2.5 cm (2 x 1 in) batten to be positioned on either side of the window reveal for hinging the shutter doors.

3 Attach four lengths of 5 cm x 12 mm (2 x ½ in) batten all around the perimeter of each cut fretwork panel, using panel pins.

4 Cut two 5 x 2.5 cm (2 x 1 in) lengths of batten to exact door height and fix them securely on either side of the window recess.

5 Fit two hinges on each fretwork panel door.

6 Fit a lever catch to the centre of the doors.

7 Mark and attach the hinges to the lengths of batten on either side of the window recess. Paint the shutters, then staple fabric to the inside of the panels for extra privacy.

FITTING BLINDS

B linds are a popular window treatment for bathrooms as they take up little room, can be highly decorative and are easy to fix in place. As a window dressing, blinds always produce an excellent finish in bathrooms. More elaborate blinds, such as Austrian and festooned types are not included here; although they can be used in bathrooms, moisture lingers in the folds of material, making them prone to damp.

Roller blinds: these are the easiest way of controlling the flow of natural light into a room. Plain or highly patterned, they can fit well into most schemes. Because they can be rolled up completely onto their retaining pole, it means that the window can be totally exposed during the day so that the maximum amount of light can be let in, which is ideal for small or dark rooms.

Roman blinds: these operate by the material being gathered upwards in folds as the blind is opened. They are slightly more complicated than roller blinds, but if plain colours are used they can have a great effect on a simple scheme.

Venetian blinds: these have always had a classical appeal because of the way in which they break up the natural light source in a variety of mood-creating ways, as well as providing total privacy when the slats on the blind are closed at night.

NO-SEWING BLINDS

It is easy to create different types of blinds very quickly, without even the hint of any complex stitching. Making a simple blind from some favourite material has never been easier, especially since the invention of touch-and-close tape.

1 Measure the exact dimensions of the window frame. Make sure the width measurements come in fractionally from the wall recesses so that the finished blind will be able to fall easily at the frame edge. Add 15 cm (6 in) onto the height measurement to allow 7.5 cm (3 in) at each end of the blind for fitting a length of wooden dowel. Mark out the material and cut it to size, using dressmaker's scissors or wallpapering scissors.

2 Cut two lengths of wooden dowel to slightly less than the window-recess width and place one at each end of the cut material. Fold over the material at one end and secure it in this position with self-adhesive touch-and-close tape. Apply the corresponding side of the touch-and-close tape 7.5 cm (3 in) further onto the material. Apply two more strips of tape in corresponding positions at the other end of the material (either side of the other batten). Fold the tape over each batten.

3 Screw two cup hooks into the window frame, in order to support the top batten while the other batten at the bottom weighs down the rest of the blind and keeps the material taut.

THE STITCHLESS LOOK
The simplest of blinds can often produce the most attractive effect. Here, the blend of colours and the intensity of the light combine to give the window a stylish finish.

PAINTING BLINDS

T he easiest way of renovating old blinds, or brightening up cheap ones, is to decorate them with a design of your own choosing. Although a number of techniques can be used to make these decorative additions, paint and fabric are the most appropriate materials to use. Roller blinds provide the best base for decoration as they are flat and they roll out into one complete 'sheet', which makes them very easy to work on.

Stencilling blinds: this is one of the quickest ways of decorating a blind. Make sure that the stencil is held firmly in place when working on fabric as mistakes are quite difficult to rectify. Mask off the area immediately above and below the stencil run, to protect it from paint-covered hands when moving the design along to the next position.

DECORATIVE TECHNIQUES

• Using paint: fabric paints should be used on blinds, although some acrylics are multi-purpose and can be used on fabric as well as walls and other surfaces. This gives the opportunity to match paint colours and texture directly between different surfaces. Stencils and stamps work particularly well on blinds, and this method of painting them also allows designs to be carried over from wall to fabric surface, creating an integrated decorative scheme in the room.

• Using fabric: cutting out different shapes or designs and using fabric glue to stick them to a plain blind is another decorative option. This technique, known as appliqué, can be very effective in transforming the look of a simple blind.

• Design tracing: colourfast ink pens are ideal for hand-drawn designs on fabric. For the less artistic, a design traced from a book or a picture can be used to excellent effect. Iron the back of the blind to 'fix' the ink once the design is finished.

Essential Plumbing

ESSENTIAL PLUMBING

Household plumbing has always been considered the domain of the professional, and this sentiment remains unchallenged for the majority of plumbing tasks around the home. However, there are some tasks that can be tackled without too much trouble: this chapter demonstrates the areas of plumbing that fit into this band of manageable jobs – tasks that either maintain systems as a whole, or involve changing fittings for a new-look bathroom. Plumbing systems vary considerably, depending on age and size requirements, so the examples given here deal with principles rather than trying to cover every eventuality. Approach plumbing work with an open mind and decide which areas you are capable of tackling and which areas should be left to the professional.

5

PLUMBING TOOLS

N ever compromise on plumbing tools as the correct ones are essential for achieving the right result. In addition to a general toolkit, the household plumber needs a few extra items. Most of these items are stocked by DIY outlets. However, for some items it may be necessary to go direct to a trade counter – this normally has the added bonus of being able to talk to an expert who can give advice.

Hole saw
For cutting pipe-sized holes through walls.

PTFE tape
Makes threaded joints watertight.

Pipe bender
For bending small-diameter copper pipes.

Pipe cutter
Makes cuts through copper or plastic pipe.

Long nose pliers
Ideal for detailed work in awkward places.

Pipe wrench
Has movable jaws to grip onto most sizes of pipe.

Adjustable pliers
Has movable jaws for maximum gripping strength.

Basin wrench
Allows easy access to tap connectors below basin.

Gas torch
For soldering pipe joints.

Plunger
For unblocking toilets and waste pipes.

CHOOSING A STYLE

T he style of fittings for a bathroom is a matter of personal taste, although it is heavily influenced by whether the bath and shower are integrated or separate, and whether the bathroom suite suits one particular type of fitting better than another. When an entirely new bathroom is being installed, most outlets supply a good range of matching plumbing. Decision-making is slightly more difficult when renovating an old bathroom suite.

Choosing a shower: showers vary considerably in price, which is due as much to design as it is to their efficiency. Make sure that the controls are simple to use and hard-wearing, and check whether the shower itself requires a complicated installation procedure, as this will increase the cost.

Basin taps: taps come in all sorts of sizes and shapes, with modern or more traditional ones being equally popular in most outlets. Always try and match the basin-tap style with those of the bath, and remember to check that the new taps you choose will fit your basin.

Integrated systems: where the bath is integrated with the shower, a simple option is to choose a telephone-style fitting with the shower head resting on a bracket above the taps. Another bracket for the shower head can be attached to the wall to allow hands-free showering.

CHANGING TAPS

O nce all the relative checks have been made to ensure that the new taps will fit your suite, exchanging them for the old ones is a relatively easy procedure. Taps are literally secured onto the end of the water pipes by simple connectors: changing them is just a matter of unscrewing these connector joints to remove the old taps, fitting the new taps in place, then screwing the connectors back in position.

1 Once the supply is shut off, you need to take off the water-supply pipe to gain access to the back nut on the tap. Use a basin wrench to undo the nut at the top of the supply pipe, which connects the pipe to the tap above.

2 With the water pipe removed, undo the tap's back nut. Repeat the process to disconnect the water pipe to the other tap. The taps are now free to be removed from above and new taps fitted. Depending on tap design, it may be necessary to disconnect the pop-up rod for the waste. This is normally a simple matter – check the manufacturer's guidelines to see whether a new basin stopper needs to be fitted.

CAUTION

Before any tap fitting can be carried out, the water supply must be turned off. Most modern water systems have shut-off valves that are situated close to the taps themselves – often they are a short way along the tap-supply pipes below the basin. The basin taps can then be turned on to drain off the small amount of water left in the end section of the pipe.

FITTING THE NEW TAPS

Washers or silicone should be
used to cushion the tap block
onto the basin surface. Check
manufacturer's guidelines for
the taps you are using.

Tap tails should be lowered through
the appropriate holes.

Washers fit onto tap tails.

Tighten the taps' back
nuts onto the tap tails
until the washers are up
against the underside
basin surface.

Tighten supply pipe nuts
onto tap tails.

To water supply.

(Only turn on water when
all joints are tightened.)

DEALING WITH LEAKING TAPS

L eaky taps are a frequent and annoying problem in bathrooms. Fortunately, they are usually an easy problem to fix, and one that takes little time and expense. The most common cause of a leaking tap is a broken or corroded washer, or one with a hairline crack. No matter what the tap design, the water must be turned off at the mains, or at the shut-off valve that feeds the tap. The tap can then be opened to drain off any water in the pipe system. Only when this is done, can you work on the tap to replace its washer.

REMOVING THE TAP HEAD

Designs vary, but in most cases the actual tap head is held on by a small grub screw, which can be undone to release the head. The screw may be hidden by a cover cap, as shown below. Once the head is removed, the internal workings are revealed. Some taps will have a further cover, or shroud, which will need to be unscrewed before you can replace the washer.

1 Flick off the cover cap with a flat-headed screwdriver, and undo the retaining screw which holds the tap head in place.

2 The washer is still hidden by the headgear of the tap. Use an adjustable wrench to grip the headgear nut and undo it slowly to remove the headgear. If the nut does not move easily and greater effort is required, make sure you support the rest of the tap with your other hand to avoid damaging any of the tap mechanism.

CHANGING THE WASHER

Once the headgear has been removed, the washer can be clearly seen, and replacing it is straightforward. In some cases, the old washer can be prised directly off the bottom of the headgear; in the example below, a small fixing nut is used to hold the washer in place.

1 Undo the fixing nut with long nose pliers. Because it is so small, this nut is easily lost so be sure to put it in a safe place before refitting.

2 Prise out the damaged washer with a flat-headed screwdriver.

3 Clip in a new washer, making sure that it is the correct size, and fits tightly in position. Refit the fixing nut and screw the headgear back into the main tap body. Once the tap head is back in place, close the tap before turning the water supply back on. If the washer has been fitted correctly, the drip will not reoccur.

5

ADJUSTING TOILET CISTERNS

T he main problems found with cisterns either involve constantly dripping overflow pipes, or insufficient water to expel all the material from the pan when the toilet is flushed. Both cases are linked to the water level in the cistern; this is easily adjustable as nearly all cistern levels are based on the same system, built around an air-filled float. This float rises and falls with the water level, shutting a valve to prevent water flow into the cistern when the water level is high, and opening the valve when water level is low (after flushing). The air-filled float is positioned on the end of an arm, and there are two main methods of adjusting the level at which the arm shuts off the incoming water flow.

Traditional ballcocks: traditional air-filled floats, often called ballcocks, can be adjusted by bending the metal arm so that the ballcock changes its level in the water. Alternatively, as shown here, its height can be adjusted by loosening a small nut which then allows the ballcock to be moved up and down a small vertical stretch of the arm, again changing its level in the water.

Plastic arms: some air-filled floats are held in position with plastic arms. In this case, adjustment tends to be at the other end of the arm, close to the valve controlling the water flow. These arms are normally adjusted by using long nose pliers to change the position of a small nut on the arm, which increases or decreases the level at which the air-filled float will shut off the water supply to the cistern.

5

BATH WASTE SYSTEMS

B ath waste systems vary considerably, but most are based on a design that takes water out of the bath through a U-bend or trap and out into the mains drainage system. Blockages and leaks occur because of problems in this simple system. Dealing with any problems is relatively simple as long as you understand the way in which such systems interconnect. This diagram shows a standard bath waste system and the areas that can cause problems.

BATH WASTE SYSTEM

Leakages can be caused by:

Holes or corrosion of the overflow seal.

The solution is to unscrew the overflow outlet system and run a bead of silicone around the exposed overflow hole before repositioning the overflow outlet system.

Holes or corrosion in the seal around the waste outlet.

The solution is to remove the waste outlet and run a bead of silicone around the exposed outlet hole before repositioning the waste outlet.

Holes or corrosion of the trap seals.

The solution is to unscrew the trap and replace the rubber seals, or use silicone sealant around the thread of the trap pipes, before screwing the trap back in position.

GENERAL MAINTENANCE

T here are many simple plumbing jobs that come under the heading of general maintenance, and these small tasks can help to keep the main elements of the bathroom functioning efficiently. Problems occur when water is either not flowing at all, or not flowing as well as it should be, and this can be the water going into the bathroom or the water coming out of it.

DESCALING A SHOWER HEAD

Most shower flow problems result from the shower head becoming blocked with mineral deposits – this is particularly common in areas with hard water. Fortunately, there is a simple way of clearing this problem and returning the shower head water flow back to its proper efficiency level.

I Unscrew the shower head to remove the perforated plate.

2 Wearing protective gloves, scrub the plate with some descaling fluid using an old toothbrush. If it is badly blocked up, soak the entire plate in a bowl of descaling fluid overnight. Rinse the plate thoroughly after it has been in contact with descaling fluid.

3 Use a pin to remove any small deposits in the perforations of the plate, but do not use this method if the plate has an integral plastic diaphragm, as this could be damaged by a pin. Reassemble the show head to see if water flow has improved.

UNBLOCKING TOILETS

Toilets are one of the more common bathroom outlets that become blocked from time to time. As soon as you notice that flushing is less efficient than normal, or waste is not being carried away with the usual ease, it is likely that a blockage is building up. It is always best to tackle the problem straight away – leave the blockage too long and major work will almost certainly be required. The solution is usually very simple.

Using a plunger: a simple plunger can often deal with minor blockages. Push it down into the bottom of the pan and work the handle up and down vigorously to create suction between the plunger head and the sides of the pan. This puts water pressure on the blockage in the pipe, which eventually shifts it out of the way.

BASIN WASTE

It is worth clearing basin waste traps from time to time as they do become blocked with small bits of debris and a build-up of silt. The design of the outlet pipe does vary, but in general there are obvious areas in the trap that are meant to be unscrewed to dispose of any debris and dirt build-up.

1 Unscrew the trap, taking care not to twist the rest of the outlet pipe structure and risk fracturing any of the seals.

2 The bottom of the trap should contain water but it ought to be relatively clean. If the water is dirty or there is debris at the bottom, clear it out then screw back the trap.

QUICK SOLUTIONS

With plumbing systems, it is always good to know how the basic system works; that way, when there is a problem, the correct course of action can be taken to put it right. In some cases, you will need to call in the professionals but there are other situations where you may be able to solve the problem yourself.

SOLVING PROBLEMS

- Corroded nuts: if you are trying to undo any pipe joints that are very stiff, try loosening them with some proprietary aerosol easing spray.
- Cold radiator: if the radiator is not giving off much heat, check that the thermostat is not broken or turned down too low. Before replacing it, bleed the radiator to make sure no air is trapped in the system, stopping the radiator from warming up. Radiators are bled using a special key that opens a valve at the top to allow trapped air to escape. Shut the valve as soon as water starts coming out. In a pressurized central heating system, take care when bleeding radiators as you may need to build the pressure back up in the system once it has been bled. Check if you need to do this in your boiler manufacturer's instructions.
- Frequent washer trouble: when washers on taps keep giving trouble, it can be due to excess mains pressure. Try turning down the mains stopcock slightly to reduce this pressure.
- Water too hot or cold: all water-heating systems have a controlling thermostat. Temperature problems with hot water can normally be traced to the thermostat, which should be adjusted as required. Check your heating installation instructions for detailed advice on thermostatic control in your system.
- Testing stopcocks: in emergencies, it may be necessary to turn off the water supply. It is vital to test stopcocks from time to time to check that they are functioning correctly; otherwise, when an emergency does arise, it may not be possible to turn the water off.
- Knowing a plumber: plumbers are well-trained professionals, and most plumbing jobs should be left to them. Find a plumber through personal recommendation, and keep the phone number handy for both emergencies and advice. Always remember that if you are in any doubt about attempting a plumbing job, it is best to call a professional.

Bath and Shower Fix-ups

Bath and Shower Fix-ups

BATH AND SHOWER FIX-UPS

The bath and shower are often neglected in a bathroom makeover because there is a feeling that, apart from replacement, there is not much that can be done to improve them. This chapter demonstrates that there are, in fact, all sorts of changes that can be made to these bathroom fittings, whether for decorative or more practical purposes. After all, looking after baths and showers has an important effect on maintaining the decorative impact of the bathroom as a whole. Finally, the ornamental aspects of decorating – those finishing touches that make a bathroom makeover complete – are considered at the end of the chapter.

TONGUE-AND-GROOVE PANELLING: 1

MAKING THE FRAME

Before the bath can be panelled, you need to build a frame onto which the panelling can be attached. Use 5 x 2.5 cm (2 x 1 in) batten for this purpose, as it is sturdy enough to provide a sound base while being easy to work with. For the best results, build a frame that combines vertical and horizontal struts, with supporting diagonal lengths to brace the entire framework and keep it firmly in position.

1 Cut some MDF that is the same width as the panelling you are going to use, to the height of the bath so that it just fits under the bath rim. Lay a piece of 5 x 2.5 cm (2 x 1 in) batten along the floor, parallel with the bath rim. Use a level and the MDF to adjust the position of the batten so that it lies directly below the bath rim. Make a pencil guideline along the batten.

2 Cut the batten to the length of the bath and screw it into the floor, using screws that are long enough to bite into the floorboards below, but not so long that they can go through the boards and damage any service pipes and wires below the floor and, more importantly, injure you.

3 Measure the height from tight under the rim of the bath to the top of the floor batten. Cut four or five pieces of batten to this length, to make vertical supports. Some baths have a horizontal batten fixed under the rim, but it may be necessary to wedge another length of batten under the rim to help fix vertical battens.

4 Fix the vertical battens at equal distances along the length of the bath, fixing at floor level and under the rim. Hold the drill at a 45-degree angle to the vertical batten and screw diagonally through it into the bottom one. When fixing below the rim, take care not to screw into the bath itself.

5 Use a mitre saw to make angled cuts in another four or five pieces of batten to use as diagonal supports. Take care when measuring these mitred lengths to fit, as they must be accurate in order to keep the frame in the correct position for attaching the panelling.

6 Fix the diagonal batten supports between all the vertical lengths of batten on the frame.

TONGUE-AND-GROOVE PANELLING: 2

O nce the panel frame has been made, the panelling must be cut to fit. Using large sheets makes the job quicker, but it is much more important that you measure them accurately as small mistakes in measurements in one area can lead to a larger mistake in another.

FITTING THE PANEL

When measuring the tongue-and-groove panelling, remember that the panel should fit just under the rim of the bath. Do not cut the panelling too large or you will not be able to get it under the rim.

1 Use a jigsaw or panel saw to cut the bath panel to size. Once in position, drill six pilot holes in the panel through to a struts beneath, one at each corner, one in the centre of the panel at the top (as shown here), and one in the centre of the panel at the bottom.

2 Screw a mirror screw into each of the pilot holes. For a totally professional finish, before inserting the mirror screw, make each hole entrance slightly larger with a countersink drill bit, so that the screw head will sit flush with the surrounding panel surface.

3 Fit a mirror screw cap to each screw. (Always remove mirror screw caps before painting the panelling and replace them once the paint has dried.)

4 For the rest of the bath surround, attach panelling as required; use panelling the same height as the bath panel itself to give a well-balanced effect. Drill pilot holes every 20 cm (8 in) along the top and bottom of the panelling into the struts beneath.

5 Use a countersink drill bit to open up the entrance to each hole before fixing the panel in place. Concrete anchor screws, which bite equally well into wood or masonry, are shown here. If you are using normal screws, insert wall plugs before fixing the screws in place.

DECORATIVE BATH SURROUND
Once painted, a tongue-and-groove panelled bath provides a decorative and hard-wearing bath surround.

6 Finally, fix a length of quadrant beading around the top of the panelling to provide a smooth finish to the edge. Decorate then seal the bath edge with silicone.

SHOWER CEILINGS

S hower ceilings are always under constant attack from moist air and can, therefore, deteriorate very quickly after decoration. Tiling a ceiling is one way of getting round this problem, although the forces of gravity make this a difficult task to achieve. Alternatively, a PVC sheet can be cut to fit the ceiling area, providing an easily cleaned, moisture-resistant surface that will not deteriorate like a painted one.

1 Measure the area directly above the shower, whether it be in a cubicle or above a bath.

2 Cut a PVC sheet to size, using a jigsaw. Remember to follow manufacturer's guidelines on safety when using a jigsaw, and at no time place any part of your body in front of the blade.

3 Apply a generous amount of silicone sealant to the back of the PVC sheet, making sure that there is plenty of sealant at the edges.

4 Press the PVC sheet into position above the shower, twisting it into place to ensure really good adhesion between the sheet and the ceiling.

5 Some screw fixings are required to fix the sheet securely. Drill pilot holes around the edge of the sheet at 20 cm (8 in) intervals, taking care when drilling into the ceiling not to damage service pipes or wires and, more importantly, not to risk injury to yourself. If you think there may be pipes or wires in the area, use a pipe and cable detector to check.

6 Insert the screws and fit plastic cover caps over them to give a neat finish. Apply a band of silicone around the edge of the PVC sheet to ensure a watertight finish.

DEALING WITH DAMP AND CONDENSATION

Damp and condensation can be a problem in bathrooms – the hot water from showers and baths is the main cause of this. An extractor fan is the best method of removing moist air from a bathroom (see page 54), but there are other measures that can also help.
- After a bath or shower, simply opening windows helps to reduce the moisture content of the air in the bathroom.

- Wiping down the moisture on walls helps to prevent the development of mould, which will always attack the decorations and lead to a rapid deterioration in their finish.
- Use proprietary bathroom paints; these are more resistant to moisture than standard varieties.
- If your windows are single-paned, consider fitting double glazing as this will reduce condensation.
- Keep the room adequately heated.

RE-ENAMELLING A BATH

R e-enamelling a bath sounds like a daunting task and, until recently, this would have been a fairly accurate sentiment, as there were no easy-to-use systems available for carrying out this recoating process. However, the situation has changed and various proprietary products are now available. Before trying one, make sure that the new enamel coating is suitable for your bath – most should only be used on previously enamelled surfaces or porcelain ones.

1 Mask all taps and other fittings on the bath with polythene sheets or bags. This has two functions: firstly, it keeps the taps clean and, secondly, it stops any drips of enamel falling on the bath surface.

2 Use an electric sander to rub down the entire bath surface. Use the finest grade abrasive paper, as you do not want to make deep cuts in the bath surface. Wear a respiratory mask while carrying out this process.

3 Clean the bath thoroughly with a mild detergent and then rinse with clean water. Allow the bath to dry completely before wiping over the surface with a cloth dampened in white spirit. This evaporates quickly to leave a totally clean bath surface ready for re-enamelling. Mask off the surrounding bath area with some masking tape.

4 Use proprietary bath enamel to spray even coats over the entire bath surface. Wear a respiratory mask while applying the enamel. Manufacturers' guidelines vary, but normally three or four thin coats will produce a good finish. Allow plenty of drying time between the coats. Remove the masking tape when the last coat has dried.

BATH RESTORATION

Re-enamelling is particularly appropriate for older roll-top baths that have suffered surface deterioration over the years. Restoring them to their original look can be a very satisfying process. The process does not have to be confined to baths – basins and shower trays can be re-enamelled as long as they have a suitable surface.

TOUCHING-IN

In many cases, re-enamelling the bath is too extreme a measure, especially if the damage is slight. Any small nicks or scrapes in a bath surface can normally be touched-in very effectively with a small paintbrush, using the appropriate colour of oil-based eggshell paint. It may be necessary to add a further coat, as it is better to apply two thin coats rather than one thick one.

SILICONE SEALING

S ilicone seals are the vital barriers that prevent any water getting through joints and cracks around all the bathroom fittings. They help to prevent damp problems that could affect the decoration in other rooms in the house, such as water leaking from the bath area and seeping through the floor and causing a damp patch on the ceiling of the room below.

REMOVING OLD SEALS

Before a new seal can be applied, the old one must be removed. The total removal of the old seal is as important as the application of the new one in ensuring a watertight finish. Leaving any of the old seal will create weak areas in the new one.

1 Cut away the old seal using a window scraper. Concentrate your efforts with the corner of the scraper along the seal itself, taking care not to scratch the bath surface. Proprietary removal fluid can be used to help the process.

2 Clean the tile/bath junction with methylated spirits, allowing it to evaporate before applying a new seal.

1

2

CARING FOR SEALS

Resealing is part of the maintenance process for a bathroom, but the life of seals can be extended by wiping them down after a shower or bath to prevent damage from standing water.

CREATING THE NEW SEAL

With a clean junction between the bath and the tiles, applying the new seal is relatively straightforward. Make sure that the diameter of the sealant nozzle is cut to a size slightly larger than the bath/tile junction.

1

2

1 Apply strips of masking tape to either side of the bath/tile junction. Run the sealant gun along the junction, keeping an even pace as this makes smoothing it much easier.

2 Use a wetted finger to run along the new silicone seal to create an uninterrupted smooth finish.

3 Remove the masking tape immediately after smoothing the silicone – do not wait until the silicone is dry before removing it.

3

ALTERNATIVE SEALS

Seals are not confined to just white tubed silicone; other alternatives may be used either for decorative or practical reasons.
- Colours: a simple change is to substitute a different colour for the existing white silicone. This colour can complement tiles or other colours in the bathroom.
- Double siliconing: where a joint is particularly large, one application of silicone may not be enough to seal

the gap effectively and neatly. Make one application to fill the deep recesses of the joint, allow it to dry then make another application – the seal will then be easier to mould into a good finish.
- Plastic seals: in areas that cause constant damp problems, you can combine plastic strip seals with silicone. Apply generous amounts of silicone sealant to the joint before applying the plastic seal over the top.

6

FINAL FIX-UPS

No bathroom makeover is complete without ornaments and all the other decorative accessories that combine to create the finished look of a new room. The decorative accessories are really a matter of personal preference, determined by the style of the room – generally speaking, plants, pictures and rugs are the favoured items. Candles are becoming an increasingly popular form of decoration, not just for bathrooms, as they can create mood through their subtle lighting and, if you use scented ones, a wonderful aroma.

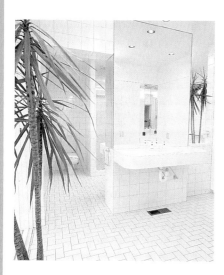

PLANTS

Pot plants bring a fresh, natural atmosphere to any room. Several plants can be clustered together or you can have a single plant with interesting foliage or bold flowers. Plants can even be chosen to complement or blend with other colours in the decorative scheme of the bathroom.

PICTURES

Your choice of pictures in the bathroom can add to the decorative effect and personalize the room. Groups of pictures, or a single painting, create focal points that help to integrate a scheme.

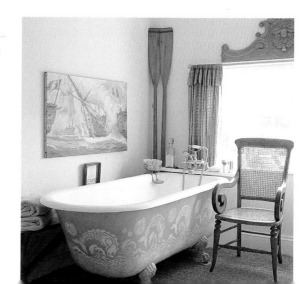

RUGS

Soft underfoot, rugs
are a popular choice
for bathrooms. Make
sure that they are dried
out after getting damp,
to prevent them from
rotting. They can be
laid over carpet, tiles
or wooden flooring. If
you are laying them
on slippery hard-tile
floors, use a suitable
non-slip backing.

CANDLES

Candles produce a
wonderful relaxed feel
in a bathroom, with
scented varieties adding
to this lovely calming
atmosphere. However,
always remember to
treat naked flames
with caution: make
sure that the candles
are not positioned too
close to curtains or any
flammable surfaces,
and never leave them
unattended.

INDEX

All illustrations by Chris Forsey. All photographs by Tim Ridley except for the following pages:

l = left, r = right, c = centre, t = top, b = bottom

Page 5b Arcaid; 7t Fritz von der Schulenberg/The Interior Archive; 8b Simon Kenny/Archaid; 12l Christopher Drake/Robert Harding Picture Library; 12r Nick Hofton/View; 13t Christopher Drake/Robert Harding Picture Library, 13b Camera Press; 30b Paul Ryan/International Interiors; 32t Paul Ryan/International Interiors, 32b Paul Ryan/International Interiors; 33 Trevor Mein/Arcaid; 41b Elizabeth Whiting & Associates; 56t Paul Ryan/International Interiors, 56b Elizabeth Whiting & Associates; 57t Elizabeth Whiting & Associates, 57b James Mortimer/The Interior Archive; 72t Elizabeth Whiting & Associates, 72b Elizabeth Whiting & Associates; 74tl Camera Press; 74tr Paul Ryan/International Interiors, 74b Fritz von der Schulenburg/The Interior Archive; 76l J.T.L. Kurtz/Camera Press, 76r Elizabeth Whiting & Associates; 77tl Camera Press, 77tr Elizabeth Whiting & Associates, 77b Simon Kenny/Arcaid; 78t Elizabeth Whiting & Associates, 78b Peter Cook/View; 84t Elizabeth Whiting & Associates, 84bl Andrew Wood/The Interior Archive, 84b Camera Press; 89tl Arcaid, 89tr David Giles/Robert Harding Picture Library, 89b Peter Cook/View; 107c Elizabeth Whiting & Associates; 110t Elizabeth Whiting & Associates, 110b Fritz von der Schulenberg/Robert Harding Picture Library.